CW00853296

Wrong Place Wrong Time

Wrong Place Wrong Time

David P Perlmutter

COPYRIGHT (C) 2013 DAVID P PERLMUTTER AND CREATIVIA

Published 2013 by Creativia
Paperback design by Creativia (www.ctivia.com)
ISBN: 1484898109
ISBN-13: 978-1484898109
The right of David P Perlmutter to be identified as author of this Work
has been asserted by him in accordance with sections 77 and 78 of the
Copyright, Designs and Patents Act 1988.
All rights reserved. No part of this publication may be reproduced, stored
in retrieval system, copied in any form or by any means, electronic, me-
chanical, photocopying, recording or otherwise transmitted without writ-
ten permission from the author.

DEDICATION

My family is such a huge part of my life and I would like to dedicate this book to them.

To Mum, for being the best Mum in the world and for never, ever failing to be there for me when I've needed you. (And boy, have I needed you!) Mum — there aren't enough words to express how grateful I am for your love, your care and your unwavering support.

To my brothers: Gary, Stuart, John and Bobby. We may not see or speak to each other as often as we should, but I want to thank you all for being there for me. I'm proud to call you my brothers, but more importantly, when people say you need just a handful of friends, to me you're 80% of that handful.

To my sister, Susan. Even though you're at least a foot shorter than me, I've always looked up to you. Thank you for the love and kindness that you've shown me over the years and for being my favourite sibling. (Just don't tell the others!)

To my four beautiful and amazing children: Stephen, Lauren, Harry and Ava. I know I haven't always been able to be there for you in person but there isn't a second that goes by when you're not in my thoughts. I want you all to know that I love you very much. Thank you for making your Dad so proud.

To my Dad. You were a complete rock to me during the period that this book represents and for that, I will be eternally grateful. Thank you. Writing this book has brought up so many memories of you; in fact it was your idea, Dad, so here it is! It's been many years since you sadly passed away but I want you to know that I think about you every day.

ACKNOWLEDGMENTS

I'd like to thank all of my family for their support and encouragement throughout my journey of writing this book, but my twin brother deserves a special mention. John designed the cover for the book and I have received so many fantastic comments about it. Thank you, John for being a creative genius. I'd also like to thank my very patient editor and friend, Elaine Denning, whom without, this book would have not have been possible. She worked her socks off day and night (she has a very strange sleeping pattern) and treated the book like it was one of her own. Thank you so much Elaine! Finally, thanks to Dan Davies for his invaluable help with formatting the book. It's very much appreciated.

- David P Perlmutter — Author

- Blog: thewrongplaceatthewrongtime.blogspot.com

- Facebook: facebook.com/wrongplacewrongtimebook

- Twitter: @davepperlmutter

- John Perlmutter — Graphic Designer www.earth8.com

- Elaine Denning — Copywriter & Editor www.wordywart.com

- Dan Davies — Kindle & eBook Formatting www.blueprintstudio.org

- Creativia — www.ctivia.com

Contents

Chapter 1

BLOW

It was a cold, bleak February afternoon in London. For the majority of it I'd been stuck in the office and liaising with clients, trying to clinch a sale on a substantial property in the West End. The potential buyer — an arrogant prick with more money than sense — was being particularly difficult, demanding that various items be left in the house before he'd commit to buy. So when the phone rang for the umpteenth time that day and he requested that the hallway mirror be a part of the deal, I almost felt like buying him one myself, just to get the deal in the bag. It had been a week of stupid, unnecessary negotiations and I couldn't wait to get the hell out of there. I called the seller, an attractive middle aged divorcee, and told her the news.

"He wants the hallway mirror."

"Oh."

"If he gets the mirror it's a done deal, Mrs Evans."

I shifted in my chair and threw some letters into my out tray. I could hear her on the end of the phone taking a long drag from her cigarette and pondering the proposition. A part of me knew she was enjoying this; enjoying the control. There were moments throughout the week when I actually thought she had no intention of selling at all and was just enjoying the attention I was giving her. I'd seen it all before and couldn't help but wonder what kind of a wanker she'd been married to.

"It's just a mirror," I told her, taking her file from the drawer.

"But a rather nice one, don't you think?" She took another drag of her cigarette and I clenched my fist, willing it to be over.

"I guess it depends who's looking into it." I flipped through the paperwork, found the prick's phone number and keyed it into the phone. "I think a mirror is only as beautiful as its beholder."

She chuckled, but said nothing.

"He has another appointment with us tomorrow," I lied. "A similar property, just around the corner from you, actually. It's a beautiful place." I tapped my fingers on the desk as Justin, my colleague, tossed his coat over his shoulder. "Mrs Evans," I said, rolling my eyes at Justin, "I really need to give him your decision now. If you lose him it could be..."

"Ok, ok," she interrupted. "He can have the bloody mirror."

"Finally!" I said, hanging up the phone. "I didn't think the cow was gonna crack!"

"Well done, mate, "Justin said, striding over to my desk with his hand in the air. I high-fived him with a grin firmly fixed on my face.

"Worked out the commission yet?" he said, heading for the door. Then he laughed. "That was a bloody stupid question, wasn't it? Come on, how much?"

"Five grand, give or take a few quid." It was a great day's work and I couldn't help but smile.

Before I left the office I called Roger, my boss, to tell him the news.

"Well done, Dave," he said. "Good work! Now get the hell out of there and get yourself a pint. You deserve it."

"I'm half way there already," I said, picking up my jacket.

"Well enjoy it." But don't go getting yourself hammered; you've got two more to settle tomorrow."

Half an hour later, I was at The Horse and Crown for a well-deserved pint. It was a small place, but substantially cheaper and more welcoming than its sister pub on the main road, which always attracted the tourists.

I was half way through my pint when Michael slapped me firmly on the back.

"Good to see you mate!" he said, slinging his jacket over the bar stool.

Mike was a good friend and a previous work colleague. We'd met several years ago when London was new to us both; when we were desperately trying to carve out our careers amongst the hardened property executives in the capital. Our grit and determination had paid off though; Mike was now a Business Development Executive with a top London firm and after three promotions I was in a very comfortable place in the same firm we had initially met.

Mike rolled up his shirt sleeves, loosened his tie and took a swig of his beer.

"So, how's life in the fast lane, mate?"

"Can't complain," I said. "Closed on a great deal just now. It took all bloody week — cute owner, prick of a buyer — but just under five k in my pocket."

"Nice one. Tonight's on you then, Dave!"

"Well, I haven't got it yet," I laughed. "I've been running around like a blue-arse fly. I've got two girls off sick so I've been covering their asses as well."

"Flu?"

"Fucking morning sickness."

Mike shook his head. "Man, you're so fucking soft. Didn't I tell you not to hire women?"

The banter continued throughout the evening and as it had been a good few months since we'd last got together, we spent quite a while in the bar chatting about work, who made the most money from our property deals and who'd had the most recent sexual encounters. It must have been after our fourth or fifth pint that we headed off somewhat inebriated to a local Indian.

We ordered our meal and a bottle of red and then proceeded to converse with a couple of girls sitting at the adjoining table. They were sisters as it turned out — Mandy and Jane — and during the course of the meal the conversation became rather flirtatious. At one point Mandy reached over and helped herself to my naan bread, and it wasn't long after that they joined us at our table. The sisters, both young, attractive girls, were like chalk and cheese. Jane was wearing a pin striped skirt suit and had her hair twisted up in a loose bun. She looked every part the PR executive she was. Mandy, on the other hand — a girl running the family horse stabling business in the West Country — was casually dressed in jeans and a t-shirt, with her long hair cascading messily over her shoulders. It was a thrown together look but it worked, and of the two, she was the one I focused my attention on. I liked her; I liked her arrogance and her 'couldn't give a shit' attitude.

The girls ate their meal — and half of ours — and when the bill had been paid it was mutually agreed that we'd head to a bar for a late night drink. As the girls had their car with them too, and had chosen a venue unknown to me, we decided to follow them in mine.

Everything was fine for the first ten minutes of the journey; we were nose to tail for pretty much most of the way, but when Mike rolled a joint and the effects of it had taken their toll, we somehow managed to lose them in the heavy, night-time traffic. We tried to find them and looked everywhere, but eventually admitted defeat. So, with little else to do, and with no desire to end the evening, Mike rolled another joint, cranked up the music and we drove around the streets of West London without a care in the world.

It must have been about half an hour later when I turned into a council estate car park. Feeling pretty invincible by then, I stupidly decided to use the car park as a Formula One racing track. Mike was far too stoned to even acknowledge where we were or what the hell I was doing; he was slumped in the passenger seat with an almighty grin on his face and just enjoying the ride. George Michael was belting out from the stereo, the windows were wound down and a cool, city breeze was keeping me alert.

I'd been driving recklessly around the car park for quite a while when two police cars with sirens and flashing lights headed towards me, stopping me in my tracks. It didn't take a genius to work out that a local resident had obviously called them, not too happy about the roaring engine and wheel spins I'd submitted them to. I quickly put my foot on the brake, turned off the music and held my breath as three coppers got out of their cars and walked towards me. One of them opened my car door and told me to get out. I obliged, and he took me to one side. I looked back at Mike but he was oblivious to it all.

The copper asked for my name, my license and then questioned what I was doing driving so recklessly in a residential area after midnight with a very real possibility of endangering someone.

What could I say? I was stoned, I was drunk. I wanted some fun. He obviously smelt alcohol on my breath because he asked if I'd been drinking.

"Just the two," I lied.

With that, he produced a breathalyser and told me to blow into the tube, and with some hesitation — as I knew I was over the limit and thinking of the consequences that would follow — I took a deep breath and did as he'd asked. After twenty seconds or so I withdrew and waited for the results with my heart skipping a beat. I was sweating profusely and sobered up quickly — very quickly. I was already regretting the night, wishing I was at home. I felt like a complete idiot.

It was just one minute later that my life turned completely upside down. The result was positive.

Almost immediately I was handcuffed, arrested, told my rights and pushed into the back seat of the police car. The drive to the station was spent sandwiched between two of them and from what I can recall I did nothing more than stare into my lap for the entire journey. Upon arrival at the station they took my belongings, fingerprinted me and then led me into a cell. I had no idea what they'd done with Mike, but to be honest, at that point he was the farthest thing from my mind.

Chapter 2

ALL FOR NOTHING

When the cell door slammed behind me, I walked over to the grubby mattress in the corner and slumped down, holding my head in my hands with my mind racing back and forth over the evening's events. I'd been so fucking stupid. Unable to settle, I stood up again and anxiously paced the floor. It seemed ironic that the cell was about the same size as the box room in the property I'd been negotiating on that afternoon. I thought of Mandy and Jane and how the hell I'd managed to lose them. I'd taken my eyes off their car for a minute — probably less than that — and as a result I was in a fucking police cell. I was scared; scared about what lay ahead, scared about my future.

Nervous exhaustion finally got the better of me and I lay on the mattress, curled up on my side with my arms folded tightly against my chest. The blanket they'd left for me did little to warm me up, but within minutes I was asleep.

It was early morning when the cell door opened. A policeman handed me a cup of coffee, his face expressionless.

"Shit," I muttered, after taking a gulp of it.

"Problem?"

"No, it's fine," I lied, wondering where the sugar was.

Normally by this time I'd have been on my way to the office and even though I detested the hour long drive in the rush hour traffic,

I'd have given anything to be behind the wheel of my car right then. No amount of hoping was going to make it happen though.

I was taken to the front desk of the station.

"You'll receive a letter in the post regarding your court case," the copper said as he put my stuff on the desk. "And we'll send you details about how to collect your car."

I nodded, gathered my things and left the station.

Outside, a cold wind wrapped itself around me, and I hurried down the street to the underground. I weaved my way through the hordes of bodies, bought my ticket at the kiosk and boarded the train. It struck me that I hadn't ridden on one for over two years and I certainly didn't want to start then. The thirty minute journey seemed endless and I couldn't wait to get out of there, so when we pulled into the station and I finally got off, it was with some relief that I made the short ten minute walk to my apartment.

As soon as I'd closed the door, I headed straight for the bathroom and turned on the shower. I stripped off my clothes, threw them on the floor and stepped under the water. I'd felt dirty all morning and it was so good to feel the crap being washed away from my body. My breath stank of stale smoke and alcohol and I grabbed my toothbrush to clean my teeth, scrubbing away the filth. As the steam filled the bathroom, I closed my eyes, lifted my face to the water and stayed there until the tension left me.

Wiping away the steam from the mirror above the sink, I was horrified. Fuck, I looked rough. My hair, in desperate need of a cut, was a mess. I pulled my fringe away from my eyes, trying to ignore the widow's peak blatantly staring back at me. Shit, I was twenty seven years old and already starting to recede. My Dad was bald but I'd always thought I'd have years before I'd have to start worrying about that. Perhaps this was the start of it? My sister always said she loved my hair; it was black, straight and shiny, and as long as hers. She said I was handsome, that I reminded her of Micheal Praed, the actor who played Robin Hood. Others told me that too, but looking at my face that morning, with the day old stubble and lack of sleep, they couldn't have been more wrong.

"Fuck," I shouted. And then "fuck" again. It all suddenly hit me. I looked at myself in the mirror, despising myself. "You fucking, stupid wanker," I said to the person staring back at me.

Once dressed and considerably calmer, I knew I had a few people to speak to, but my first call had to be to my parents. I nervously dialled their number wondering who would pick up. It was Mum that answered.

Somehow I managed to relay the story to her and felt terrible when she started to cry. She told me how stupid I'd been and when the tears subsided she said that I had to phone my boss immediately to explain what had happened.

"Pray that you've still got a job, darling," were her parting words.

I made a strong, black coffee, took a deep breath, and dialled my Manager's direct line.

"Good morning, Roger speaking, can I help you?"

"Morning Roger, it's Dave. I need to see you today. It's urgent, I'm afraid. And..." I hesitated "...it's rather sensitive."

"No problem!" he said, and then paused. "You're not resigning are you?" He laughed; completely unaware of what was to come.

"No," I told him. "Is three ok?"

"Sure, Dave, I'll see you then."

I hung up the phone.

By half past three I had lost my job.

I gave back the car keys and told Roger that the car was in the compound in Camden. I handed back the office keys and was told to clear my desk before close of business that today. As Roger pointed out in the contract he retrieved from my file, any employee who loses their driving licence under the influence of alcohol would automatically, and with immediate effect be dismissed from their position. I was gutted to learn that I'd only receive one month's salary and all the commission due to me — including the recent five grand — was not going to be forthcoming.

Roger thanked me for my services over the past few years, shook my hand and wished me luck for the future.

"Oh, and Dave?" he said, as I was halfway out the door.

"Yes?"

"You're a fucking idiot."

I closed the door behind me, walked down the stairs and out of head office onto the busy London streets. That's the last time I'll leave that building I thought to myself as I negotiated my way through the people and headed down to the underground. I paid for a ticket and boarded the train with the words "you're a fucking idiot" ringing in my ears.

That evening, I visited my parents. They were more upset than angry; they could see how I was feeling and didn't have to tell me what an arsehole I'd been. I phoned Mike that evening too, and told him what had happened. He was sorry, but what more could he say? I told him I'd catch up with him soon and finished the call. I really wasn't in the mood for talking.

My court appearance followed within a matter of days which resulted in a twelve month driving ban and a hefty fine. I'd had it all: an excellent career and salary with a smart BMW and a luxury apartment. But I lost everything in one stupid, reckless evening. Not being able to afford the payments on my apartment, my parents suggested that I move back in with them. Although I was more than appreciative of their support, depression quickly set in when it hit me that I'd just kissed goodbye to my salary, my home and the lifestyle I'd loved.

I spent the next few months staring at a TV screen and feeling extremely sorry for myself, refusing to go out and refusing to face up to the situation. I became a complete recluse and hated myself for it.

I needed some breathing space to get away from it all and to re-evaluate my life, so, with nothing better to do, I decided to take some time out. I booked a one way ticket to Spain where I planned to spend the summer. A trip to clear my head seemed like my very best option.

The night before I left, my family arranged a small party for me.

Actually, it was more of a get together considering that losing my job, home and driving license wasn't cause to get the party poppers out.

We were a very close family; four brothers and a sister. I had a twin brother, John, but we were like chalk and cheese. He was arty and extremely clever, whereas I was sporty and now, it seemed, fucking stupid as well.

The champagne flowed that night. Okay, I lie, it was sparkling wine, but it was a lovely evening, albeit rather emotional. Just before midnight the family started to say their goodbyes and head for home. My youngest brother, Bobby, gave me a hug at the door.

"For fuck's sake Dave," he said, "look after yourself, eh? And don't get into any trouble."

"Me?" I replied.

"Yes you, ya bastard. Just be careful."

I smiled. "Course I will mate. Now piss off and leave me to pack."

There were hugs all around from John, Stuart and Gary, my eldest brother. They all wished me good luck and told me to stay in touch. Then followed a huge hug from my sister, Susan. For as long as I could remember I'd always called her Pink, but to this day I have no idea why.

"Please Dave, take care," she said, squeezing me tightly.

"Don't worry Pink, I will," I promised her.

"Good, because you've put Mum and Dad through enough already."

"Yeah, yeah I know."

She leaned into my face and kissed me, then headed down the path after our brothers.

I thanked Mum and Dad for the party and headed to the spare room where I'd been sleeping for the past few months. My empty suitcase was on the bed beckoning to be filled, and just as I was about to start packing there was a faint knock on the door. I turned round to see my Mum standing there.

It couldn't have been easy bringing up six children, but Mum had always been there for us all. She was warm, kind hearted and did all she could to take care of us. You'd have thought that with the demands of having such a large family to look after, her physical appearance may have taken a back seat. But far from it; she was always immaculately dressed. She looked lovely that night.

"Do you need any help, darling?"

I shook my head. "Don't fuss Mum. I can do it. But thanks."

She smiled, nodding her head, and closed the door quietly behind her.

I finished packing and got into bed. Lying there, with my arms behind my head, I was excited about getting out of London and my miserable day to day existence. I thought of the sun, the sea and the sand and of the women I hoped I'd meet. And before I knew it, Mum was knocking on the door the following morning with a cup of coffee — with sugar this time — and a few slices of toast. Every morning without fail she had breakfast ready for me, even though I always told her I could do it myself. She wouldn't have dreamed of letting me do it though, and twenty-one years on, that still brings a smile to my face.

Chapter 3

EL VIAJE

My flight was at one in the afternoon and my parents insisted on driving me to Gatwick Airport. I put my suitcase in the boot of the car and we left the house three hours early to make sure I arrived on time. It was pouring down and we thought there would be heavy traffic, especially at that time of the morning. The conversation in the car was light-hearted, interspersed with my parents' concern that I look after myself.

"Please call us as soon as you get there," Mum said.

"Don't worry, I will, "I promised.

I was feeling excited and happy for the first time in months and the journey flew by in a flash.

Once at the airport we said our goodbyes.

"Dave, have a great time," Mum said, "but please be careful, okay?"

I sighed. "Mum, I'll be fine! Stop worrying!" I wrapped my arms around her. "But thanks. I love you."

I pulled away and faced my Dad, knowing he was sure to have some words of wisdom for me.

"Son, have fun," he said. "But behave. Don't do anything stupid."

I nodded.

"Just watch out for the cops," he went on. "Some of them are cunts."

I was a bit taken aback. I'd never heard him swear before. He used the occasional 'sod' or 'bloody' on a particularly bad day, but nothing quite as extreme as the c word. He hugged me and planted a firm kiss on my cheek.

"I'll be fine, Dad," I told him.

I opened the boot, grabbed my case, said my final goodbyes and made my way to the building, turning to wave as I reached the door.

Thankfully there wasn't much of a queue at the check-in desk. An attractive redhead said hello and politely asked for my passport. I handed it over with a smile.

"Do you have any luggage, sir?"

"Here you go," I told her, and placed my case on the conveyer belt. She attached a few stickers and I watched as it disappeared through the rubber flaps.

"Thank you, sir. Your flight will be called in about an hour. Have a good trip!"

"Thanks!" I replied with a grin and a cheeky wink, and made my way to the departure lounge. I was feeling good — very good — and couldn't wait to get there.

Before long I boarded the plane and saw that I had a window seat next to a nice, elderly couple. The captain introduced himself and his crew, and then announced that we'd be arriving in Spain in just over two hours. The weather, he told us, would be twenty eight degrees. Everybody on the plane cheered because outside the rain was hammering against the windows. I thought of my parents momentarily, hoping they'd be safe on their journey home, and as we took off I peered out through the tiny square window and watched the bedraggled airport staff going about their work, trying to shield themselves from the downpour. As the countryside receded into a grey, lifeless sky and the cars on the motorways became nothing more than dots, I smiled. I was getting away from it all and I couldn't have been happier.

After a decent flight, we landed at Malaga Airport with the heat of the late afternoon sun hitting me as soon as I stepped off the plane.

We were driven by the waiting bus to the baggage collection area and before I knew it I was passing through passport control. At last; I was in Spain!

I whistled for a taxi and asked the driver to take me to Marbella. To this day I don't know why I ended up there. I was somewhat aware of its reputation (Costa del Crime) but this didn't hold me back. I'd also heard a lot about Puerto Banus, a glamorous place not far from Marbella, and thought it would be worth a look.

The taxi driver told me in broken English that it would take around forty-five minutes to get to Marbella but we actually got there much sooner. I'd heard about the reputation of the Spanish drivers — especially those making a living from airport fares — so I was glad to arrive in the centre of the town in one piece.

I wandered around the town feeling free; as if a huge weight had been lifted from my shoulders. There I was in Marbella, the sun was shining and wherever I looked there were women scantily clad in bikinis and sarongs, strolling around looking beautiful. There were a few casual glances in my direction, a few reciprocated smiles and I felt good. I felt really good.

For my first night I decided to treat myself to a decent hotel as, after all I'd been through, I thought I deserved a bit of luxury. When I noticed a beautiful building in the distance, looming up from within a circle of palm trees and standing prouder than the rest, I made my way there. The building was modern, clean and crisp and situated close to the beach, bars and restaurants. It was a four star and looked a lot grander than it had from a distance, but I figured I could afford a couple of nights there until the need to find much cheaper accommodation would become a necessity.

The woman behind the reception desk looked up.

"Ola!" I said. "Do you have any rooms available for two nights?" I intended saying 'please,' but "por favor" left my mouth instead.

Not bad, Dave... not bad at all! I muttered to myself.

She replied in Spanish and I looked blankly at her. I knew I should have learned the language! "Sorry?" I said rather embarrassingly.

She sighed, and her shoulders seemed to lift and fall in annoyance. "I have a double room available," she said in perfect English, rolling her eyes at me.

What a bitch! I thought. "I'll take it," I told her. It was a lot more than I wanted to pay, but determined not to make a complete ass of myself I decided to stay just for the night.

She asked for my passport, took a photocopy and handed me a form to complete. I paid in cash and she handed back my passport with the key to my room, number 373. I took the lift to the third floor then walked through a maze of corridors until I found it. The room was beautifully decorated. It had a huge king sized bed, an ensuite bathroom and a spacious balcony with a stunning sea view. When I saw a phone by the bed I decided to make a quick call to my parents to get it out of the way. The answer machine clicked in almost straight away.

"I am sorry; there is no one home at the moment. Please leave a message after the beep and we will get back to you on our return. Thank you."

I chuckled. Mum's voice always sounded like the Queen's on the machine. It was so posh; it was a running family joke.

"Hi Mum, hi Dad, it's me. I'm here and I'm fine. Speak soon, love you!" I was about to hang up but lifted the receiver back to my ear. "And please," I said, "don't worry!"

After unpacking some of my clothes I stripped down to my boxers and located the mini bar. Out on the balcony I unscrewed the small bottle of whisky I'd taken and raised the bottle to the sea. "Cheers!" I said, and drank it in one go. I had another, wallowing in the sunshine with the rays beating down on my pasty, white body. A couple of hours later, considerably more relaxed, I took a shower, changed and headed out to see what the nightlife had in store for me.

My first night in Marbella took me to some of the local hotspots and it dawned on me pretty quickly that keeping a low profile would be a sensible option, as it came to my attention that there were some rather unsavoury characters in the area. I'd always considered myself a streetwise guy from London, but this wasn't my patch and I realised I could easily get out of my depth if I wasn't careful.

After visiting some local bars, drinking a few cocktails and feeling pretty damn good, I came across a Karaoke bar. It was filling up and I could hear from the street a guy singing a Frank Sinatra song; My Way. He had an incredible voice — far too good for karaoke — so I ventured inside to check him out. It turned out that he was the main act for the evening and that the Karaoke would start after he'd finished his set. I found a space at the bar, pulled up a stool, sat down and ordered a Bacardi and coke. The barman tossed a couple of ice cubes into a tall glass, poured my drink and put it in front of me.

"There you go," he said.

I recognized the accent straight away; he was a cockney through and through. I thought I'd strike up a conversation with him, thinking perhaps he'd be from my neck of the woods.

"So where are you from?" I said, handing him a note.

"What?" he replied, staring at me.

I thought perhaps he hadn't heard me over the music. "Where are you from?" I shouted.

He glared at me. "Who wants to know?"

"Just asking where you're from, that's all. I took a sip from my drink. And then he flipped.

"Why the fuckin' questions?"

"Hey, sorry, man," I said, holding my hands up. "Just trying to be friendly!"

"Well don't. Or your break won't be just your fuckin' holiday, but your fuckin' legs an' all."

It turned out that he was the owner and was running the bar along with his son. I also worked out pretty quickly that he didn't appreciate general chit chat. I strolled away from him to the end of the bar and pulled up a stool. Why I decided to stay escapes me now, but after a few more drinks, my wisdom and common sense flew out of the window together with my sobriety.

When the evening's main act had come to an end, it was the turn of the drunken wannabe singers to belt out their tunes. And before I knew it I was up, gaining a higher profile than should have been sensible considering the circumstances, and singing my heart out.

The main act in the bar was run by a hard man double act. Kelvin the singer, who'd sang the Frank Sinatra song earlier, was an ex-army chap who told me afterwards about his time in Northern Ireland. Anthony, his brother, arranged the music. A George Michael in the making I was not, but for some reason they took to me. After a couple of songs and a bit of a laugh about my mediocre performances, they seemed to like me.

"So Dave, when did you arrive?" Kelvin asked in his broad, Midlands accent.

"Just today," I said. "I'm here for the summer."

"Cool! We've been here for three months now. "You'll love it! The fucking birds are right up for it!"

I couldn't help but laugh.

"Where're you staying"? Anthony asked.

"A hotel up the road. It costs a bloody fortune though, so it's just for tonight."

"What are you doing here?" he said. "Working?"

"No, nothing," I told him. "I haven't got any plans at all. I don't even know my way around yet!"

To my complete surprise they offered me some part time work. To start with they said I could help out with setting up the equipment, and then once I got to know the area a bit better I could spend time trying to get them some extra gigs. The cash would definitely come in handy, I thought, and it would be a great opportunity to get my name around the place. Perhaps I'd even be able to extend my trip? I accepted their offer immediately and ordered another round of drinks.

"Cheers, guys," I said, "this is a great help."

"No sweat, Dave, Anthony said. "We need it. And we know how it is when you're alone in a place you haven't been to before."

Once the gig was over and the gear had been dismantled and packed away, a group of girls wandered into the bar. There were five of them, all from England and all rather attractive. We established more or less straight away that this was their last night in Marbella after a fortnight's holiday, and they intended to see it out with a bang. It didn't take long to get acquainted and before long we were buying them drinks and having a great time. My conversation with one girl in particular became very flirtatious and we moved away from the rest of the group. Her name was Emma. She was twenty-two, dark haired, tall, slim and curvaceous. It occurred to me that my first night — and her last night — in Spain could perhaps end far better than I could have hoped for.

Sometime later, with Emma and I becoming a little too intimate for a public place, we decided to walk back to the hotel. We were heading out of the bar, hand in hand, when I heard my name being called.

"Oi, Dave!"

I turned around. It was Kelvin, shouting across the bar. "Yeah man, what's up?"

"Meet me and Anthony at the beach bar at two tomorrow. We need a chat about the next gig."

"Yeah, sure," I said. "Where is it, mate?"

"Right at the beginning of the beach front. You can't miss it. Chico's."

"Original name," I shouted back, laughing.

"Yeah, I know," he said. "See you then, mate."

I opened the door for Emma and started to follow her through.

"Oi, Dave!" I heard again. I turned around, rather impatiently this time, keen to get Emma back to the hotel.

"I told you about the girls, didn't I?" he said, raising his glass in the air.

I was thankful that I'd booked the four star because Emma was certainly impressed. We were both pretty drunk already, but back at the room I wasn't ready for the night to end.

"So babe," I said, "fancy another drink?"

"Yeah sure," she said. "It's my last night. May as well make the most of it!"

She kicked off her shoes as I pulled two vodkas from the mini bar. I perched on the edge of the bed where she was stretched out, propped up on one elbow.

"Cheers!" she said, grabbing the drink and downing in it one. She cleared her throat, blinked her glassy eyes a few times and said: "wow that was strong!"

I laughed. "Fancy another?"

"Yeah, why not, go on then," she said, smiling.

She drank the second one just as quickly, tossed the empty bottle onto the floor and looked into my eyes. "Are you trying to get me drunk, Dave?" She giggled.

"Me?" I said. "Never!" And with that, her lips were on mine, her arms were wrapped around my neck, and she was pulling me onto the bed. Judging by the way her back was arching and the way she was thrusting her hips towards my hand, she was more than ready for me. Our clothes were off within seconds, we were kissing each other passionately, and I thrust myself into her like it was the most natural thing in the world.

We made love twice that night and sometime just before sunrise we drifted off to sleep with our legs entwined, her head on my chest and with nothing more than a sheet draped over us.

The following morning I awoke to bright sunlight streaming through the balcony doors. Emma was still wrapped in my arms and fast asleep. I turned my head to look at her. Even after a heavy night and only a few hours sleep she looked gorgeous; her make-up had long gone but she was naturally beautiful with long eyelashes, flawless skin and full lips. I gently kissed her neck, running my fingers through her hair, and when she opened her eyes and smiled at me, I smiled back.

"Morning, handsome!" she said, propping herself up.

"Morning, sexy!" I linked my arm around her waist, pulling her towards me, and with no hesitation at all she straddled me.

We kissed and made love again with sunlight bathing the bed. It was an amazing start to the day. As much as I could have stayed there for the rest of the morning, time wasn't on our side. Emma had a plane to catch back to the UK, so after a shower, a quick coffee and a brief chat about the places she thought I should visit, we said our farewell.

I knew I had to vacate the room by midday, so I threw my clothes into my case and headed down to reception. There was a man behind the desk and I handed him the key, glad the bitch from the previous evening wasn't there.

"Thanks amigo," I said, picking up my case. I headed across the foyer but he called after me.

"Sir! Wait! You have bill to pay. You make call to UK yesterday?"

It had completely slipped my mind. "I'm sorry, yes," I said, reaching for my wallet.

He handed me the bill and I cringed.

"For one call? It was a bloody answerphone!" I said.

"Sorry Sir," he muttered.

"Shit!" I said under my breath, tipping a handful of change onto the desk. I thumbed through the notes left in my wallet and realised I'd spent far too much already — including the hotel and the drinks, it was half the amount I had arrived with. The thought of going back home broke in less than a week with my tail between my legs just didn't bare thinking about.

I went through the revolving glass doors and stepped into the street, thoughts of Emma still on my mind. It had certainly been a room to remember, but not one I was likely to visit again. It suddenly occurred to me that I hadn't paid for the mini bar drinks and so I dashed across the street as fast as I could and didn't look back.

Wandering around in the midday sun was, in one way, an absolute pleasure considering the weather I'd left behind in London. But dragging a heavy suitcase from one place to the next and searching for somewhere to stay which was within my dwindling budget wasn't an ideal situation to be in. It didn't, however, take me long to find somewhere. It was in a three story Georgian style building, situated within a delightful square and surrounded by orange grove trees.

And as it was only a ten minute walk to the main strip in Marbella,
I couldn't have asked for a better location. The owner of the hostel
— who was very welcoming — showed me the room. It was basic;
nothing more than a single bed, a shower, a wardrobe and a bedside
table, but it was cheap. I quickly agreed to take it.

What more could I have asked for? I had a room in a great location,
right by the sea. I was surrounded by beautiful women. The climate
was perfect and I'd already found myself a part time job. For the first
time in months it felt like everything was beginning to fall into place.

Chapter 4

BROTHERS IN ARMS

I threw on shorts and a shirt, slipped my feet into my flip flops and headed out the door. There was almost an hour to spare until I had to be at Chico's to meet Kelvin and Anthony, but not wanting to miss a moment of the sunshine I thought I'd take a stroll along the beach front. My head was still banging from the night before and every step vibrated right through my body, but it was nothing a swim in the sea wouldn't sort out. It was amazing to think that only twenty four hours before I'd been at home in the pouring rain.

I could see from the top of the hill that the beach was crowded with people and I couldn't wait to be amongst them. I quickened my step and within minutes the white paving beneath my feet gave way to sand. The view was beautiful: a crystal clear sea glistening beneath the blazing sun and a long stretch of powder white sand, shaded by palm trees, sweeping off into the distance. A gorgeous mix of salt water and sun tan lotion wafted around me and I breathed it all in, smiling to myself. To the left of me was a strip of bars, shops and restaurants and I spotted Chico's immediately. As Kelvin had said, it was right at the beginning of the beach front. To my surprise, the guys were there already, sitting at a table with a blonde in a bikini. I made my way over, taking in the vast array of beautiful topless women as I passed them. Later, Dave, I told myself, with a smile on my face.

The bar looked more like a hut; a low-rise rectangular building made entirely with logs. It had a huge, wooden deck at the front making a great terrace that housed about ten or twelve tables. Most of them were full and there were people propping up the bar at the far end, too. As stupid and unoriginal the name 'Chico's' was, it was certainly a busy place.

I walked up to the three of them and shook hands with the brothers.

"Good night then?" Kelvin asked with a smirk on his face.

"Amazing mate! She was as sexy as fuck. Great in bed!"

Kelvin grinned. "That's my man!" He held his hand in the air and snapped his fingers, beckoning the waiter. One appeared within seconds.

"Tres cervezas, por favor. And the usual for Anja," he said.

This was obviously their local, and who could blame them? It was in a perfect setting. There was a girl to my right who'd been looking our way ever since I arrived and I couldn't help but hope she'd been looking at me. This definitely seemed like the place to be.

Kelvin was the stud of the two brothers. I learned later that Anthony hadn't met a girl in the entire time he had been there. At first I couldn't understand it because he was quite a good looking guy, but he was definitely the quieter of the two and didn't have much to say for himself.

The waiter brought our order over on a tray and placed the drinks on the table.

"Gracias" we said, almost in unison, and laughed.

I picked up my San Miguel, took a deep breath and blew out through my mouth. I was as thirsty as hell, but wasn't sure a beer was the sensible option.

"Oh come on, mate," Kelvin said. "Hair of the dog. You're on holiday!"

"You're right," I said. "Sod it. Salud!" I clinked glasses with the others, took a long swig from the bottle and felt the cold, amber liquid slide down my throat. Perhaps it was just what I needed after all?

The blonde sitting next to Kelvin was stunning; I couldn't take my eyes off her. She had shoulder length hair, a deep, chestnut tan, and bright blue eyes. Her body looked fantastic in her two piece swimsuit and she noticed me staring at her as she sipped her vodka and orange. But she wasn't the only one who had clocked my interest.

"Dave, this is Anja," Kelvin said. "She's my girlfriend." He emphasised the 'girlfriend' syllables, making it clear exactly who she belonged to.

"Hi Anja, pleased to meet you!" I said, looking straight into her delicious eyes. God, she was beautiful.

"Ola Dave," she said, leaning over Kelvin to kiss me on both cheeks.

"So, what's the score tonight?" I said to Kelvin, trying my best to divert my eyes from Anja.

"We've got a gig at Bar Lolita, just up the road from the one last night. I'll be singing from around ten, so if you can get there by eight you can hand out some leaflets to get the punters in."

"Excellent." I said. "I can't wait!"

"You can help me set up, too," Anthony added, almost as an afterthought.

"No problem, mate," I told him.

"Did you find a cheaper room Dave?" he went on monotonously.

The poor guy sounded like he was about to slit his wrists; it was no wonder that he hadn't pulled a bird yet. "Yep!" I told him. It's only a small place in a hostel up the road, but it's so cheap, I couldn't say no!"

"That's great!" Kelvin said.

"It's very good, ya!" Anja reconfirmed in her sweet, Swedish accent.

We finished our drinks and Kelvin slipped a couple of notes onto the table. "Right Dave, gotta go," he said. "We've got a lot on today."

"Ok, I'll see you at eight then," I said.

"Don't be late," Anthony piped up.

I tried to hide my annoyance. "Don't worry, boss," I said. "I'll be there."

I watched the three of them as they made their way across the deck and onto the beach. I couldn't help but notice that Anja, walking hand in hand with Kelvin, had one hell of a sexy wiggle.

Not surprisingly, I felt rather tipsy after my first beer. Having not eaten anything, and still hungover, lunch seemed like a sensible option.

"Uno cerveza, por favor," I told the waiter. "And... umm... a ham and cheese toasty." I hadn't yet established what a ham and cheese toasty was in Spanish.

I glanced to my right to see if the girl who was looking over towards our table earlier was still there, but she'd left. In her place was a table full of guys sipping beer.

I turned to face the beach. Half naked girls and men in speedos and shorts were sunbathing. There were couples playing bat and ball on the sand and lots more splashing around in the sea. I watched them as I ate my sandwich, keen to get down there and join them.

When the bill arrived I was astounded; it was far more than I expected it to be. It was amazing how quickly my memories of England seemed to be leaving me — after all, I'd worked in property for years and knew a good location was where the money was, but even so, Marbella was almost off the scale. I was thankful to be earning some much needed cash later that night.

Strolling across the sand towards the sea, I couldn't get over the vast array of tits on display. Big, small, firm and saggy — they were everywhere! Thankfully the tide was out, so it took a while to reach the shore. Once down at the water's edge, I threw my t-shirt onto the sand and ran, then dived, straight into the sea. It was freezing — so cold it almost took my breath away — but totally refreshing. I stayed there until the pounding in my head had subsided, swimming around for a while enjoying the view, and then I settled back on the beach to dry off.

It was late afternoon when I decided to return to my room for a siesta. The ten minute walk back up the hill practically finished me off, and I slept for a couple of hours, finally waking at seven. I grabbed a quick shower, slipped on jeans and a white shirt, and made my way to Bar Lolita to meet Kelvin and Anthony.

I spent the first few minutes of the evening standing on the street corner and handing out leaflets to passers by, but it soon occurred to me that if I wanted to make some decent money I'd have to put in more of an effort. Commission was being paid to the guys on bar takings, so I did my very best to get people through the door. To be honest it was a walk in the park. It was a million miles away from negotiating high end property deals but the premise was the same: I had to use my charm. Being a people's person, it didn't take much out of me — in fact I quite enjoyed it. A few guys took the piss, but on the whole everyone was friendly and willing to give me a few minutes of their time. To be honest, I'd have done it for free — there were some great looking girls out that night, and as it was my intention to have a laugh, a few drinks and perhaps hook up with one of them, I couldn't have asked for a better start to the evening.

Kelvin and Anthony were propping up the bar when I walked in.

"Hi guys," I said, "all done."

"You gave them all out, yeah?" Anthony questioned. "We need a lot of punters in tonight, Dave."

"Yes mate; I got rid of the lot. It should be pretty packed." There was something about him that was really beginning to piss me off. He'd never been in a position of authority before and it seemed like this new job role as 'my boss' was going straight to his head. My old boss, Roger, managed a multi-million pound portfolio and even he didn't nag as much as Anthony did.

"Right, time for a drink," Kelvin said, gesturing to the barman.

"I'll get these," I told him. I didn't have a great deal of money left but I knew more money would be coming my way at the end of the night.

"I'll have a pint," Anthony said almost immediately. "And get Kelvin a brandy."

For a quiet bloke, he didn't half talk a lot.

"Kelvin," I said, putting the change in my pocket, "what are you singing tonight?"

"West End Girls, Wild Boys... you know, all the eighties ones. I'll follow up with some more recent stuff."

"Love it!" I said. "I'm such an eighties guy." It may have been 1991, but my heart was still stuck in the decade before.

Kelvin laughed. "Yeah mate, I can tell that by just looking at your bloody haircut!"

"You can talk!" I retaliated.

We had another couple of drinks and by ten the bar was pretty full. As Kelvin was singing his first number, Anthony approached me at the bar.

"Dave, if you carry on getting this amount of punters in, I'll be out of a job," he said.

"Don't be silly, mate," I told him. "The job's yours. Your brother needs you far more than he needs me." I patted him on the shoulder, wanting to give him a bit of confidence.

As Kelvin was finishing his song Anja arrived, and fucking hell, she looked amazing. She was wearing a white cotton summer dress which set off her tan perfectly and her loose, blonde hair was falling over her shoulders. Every bloke in the bar stared at her; in fact most of the women did as well. She looked stunning. Anthony was on his way to the stage to put on the next track and greeted her with a kiss as she passed him. She waved, smiled and blew a kiss to Kelvin too, and he smiled and winked back at her. Then she made her way to the bar and kissed me on both cheeks.

"Ola Dave, you look nice!" She said it in a way that I took as being nothing other than friendly.

"Thanks Anja," I said. "You don't look so bad yourself!" I looked her up and down but immediately told myself to get a grip. She was Kelvin's girlfriend and completely out of bounds. I bought her a drink — as if I had a never ending supply of money — and we turned around to watch Kelvin on the stage. He definitely looked the part up there and had a great voice. I could see what she saw in him.

After a couple of numbers and a few more drinks, I moved to another part of the bar and struck up a conversation with a couple of guys from Manchester. As they were wearing football shirts it was obvious they were fans of the game, as was I, and it was because of that that I approached them in the first place. In hindsight, I shouldn't have bothered.

"I hate fuckin' Liverpool," the guy said, swaying on his feet and spilling beer on the floor. He took another mouthful, dribbling some of it down his chin. "Fuckin' scousers."

"I fuckin' hate 'em , too," his mate piped up. "We drew one all with 'em last week, the lucky bastards. I was there. Had a fight. It was great."

When Anthony called me from the other side of the bar, I couldn't have been more relieved.

"United! United" they sang, as I made my excuses and left.

"This is Marbella, not fucking Tenerife," one of the barmen said, shaking his head as I passed him.

I helped Anthony clear Kelvin's equipment away and then got set up for the Karaoke. The night went well and many people got up to sing. Some were pretty good, some were completely hopeless; but it was entertaining nevertheless. As Anthony manned the change of songs requested by the punters, Kelvin, Anja and I sat at the bar, chatting and laughing. Anja and I got on really well; it was nothing flirtatious, we were just being friendly. Anyway, I kept telling myself, she was Kelvins girlfriend. I had no inclination or desire to step on his toes.

It had been a long night, but a success, and Anthony and I packed away the last of the equipment with my energy level dwindling rapidly. I was completely knackered and I'd had enough. It was time to call it a night.

"Guys, I'm whacked," I said, sitting on a stool with both of my elbows on the bar.

"Oh come on Dave," Kelvin pleaded. "Have another drink." He reached into his pocket and pulled out a wad of notes. "Here ya go, mate. Thanks for your help tonight."

"Thanks," I said.

"Yes, Dave, please stay for another drink," Anja said, smiling at me.

I noticed the look Kelvin gave her; he obviously wasn't very happy with her input to the conversation.

"Okay, okay," I surrendered with my hands in the air. "Just one more, but it's on me." I ordered four brandies, a drink for the barman, and handed him the cash. I downed my drink in one and stood up. "Right you bastards, I'm off. See you tomorrow at Chico's."

I staggered out of the bar and made my way up the hill to my room, cursing myself. I'd just spent a fortune on one round of drinks and had walked out with less money than I'd walked in with, even after being paid.

Over the following days whilst helping Kelvin and Anthony set up their equipment at various bars and venues, I began to get to know the area and made some friends along the way. I was having the time of my life, chilling out on the beach by day and partying by night. I was getting paid regularly and was now earning enough cash to keep me going — to help pay for my room, drinks and food. Perhaps more importantly, I was gaining popularity, meeting girls and enjoying the attention and the sex. I was really becoming a part of the scene; even the unsociable owner of the first bar I'd gone into was now welcoming me into his establishment with open arms. I was bringing him customers, so no wonder his attitude had changed.

Not so long before, I'd been the new kid on the block. But now I was part of a group who people came to see and wanted to be friends with. Strangers would say hello and chat to me as if they'd known me for years, buying me drinks at each bar we worked in. I couldn't wander around the town without being stopped for a chat. I was asked how I was, and I was told if I needed any help, people would be there for me. I felt good. Actually, I felt great. I was having the time of my life.

Kelvin, Anthony and I developed a bit of a routine: we would meet for breakfast, then go to the beach and spend the day deciding on the order of songs he would sing. We'd arrange for the equipment to be delivered and set up by a certain time, and then we'd meet at the bar to ensure everything was in order. Kelvin would sing and Anthony and I would deal with the music. Then, once Kelvin completed his set, we would arrange the Karaoke and let the customers have their turn with the microphone. Every night there was plenty to drink and plenty of women. I loved it.

There was one night in particular that didn't go to plan. Kelvin and Anthony were both up on the stage while Anja and I were at the bar, enjoying the music. We'd all had a fair bit to drink, the atmosphere was pumping and I guess Anja was being a little friendlier with me than usual. She was a beautiful girl, I was flattered by her attention, and although I did nothing to provoke it, I guess I didn't do enough to stop it either. I was completely aware that she was Kelvin's girl — the guy who had given me an opportunity on my very first night — and I completely respected that. At one point Kelvin's eyes met mine and I could tell he wasn't happy, but he was in the middle of a song and there was little he could do. Knowing that Kelvin had a jealous streak and a very short fuse, I was beginning to feel uncomfortable.

The guys finished their set, left the stage and joined us at the bar. I could tell straight away that Kelvin still had a problem and wasn't prepared to let it go. I have to admit that I'd found him to be rather intimidating, right from the first moment he'd told me about his army life in Northern Ireland.

"Oi, Dave, stop fucking with me," Kelvin said, rather aggressively.

"Sorry?" I replied.

"You know what I mean. I've seen you chatting up Anja."

"Kelvin, don't be stupid mate. I'd never do that."

"I've seen you, you cunt," he went on, getting up from his stool.

He was the same height as me but had a more muscular physique. My instincts kicked in. I tried to defend myself in a calm and reasonable way, protesting at how ridiculous the accusations were. But he wasn't the type to appreciate civilized communication.

"Calm down, mate, you've got this all wrong." I stood up, backing off.

"I am not your fucking mate," he spat.

Anja tried to intervene. "You're being pathetic Kelvin, "she said. He's done nothing wrong!" But this just made matters worse.

"Yes he has," Anthony piped up. "I've seen him trying it on with her, Kel."

Well that's just fucking great, I thought. Now his dimwit of a side-kick was in on the act: defending his brother, accusing me, pointing at me, shouting in my face and pushing me. The situation was getting seriously out of hand.

Before I even had time to plot my next move, Kelvin took a swing at me. His left fist connected with my chin, his right with my eye. He caught the bridge of my nose and splatters of blood landed on my shirt. I heard Anja pleading with Kelvin to stop, but Anthony was alongside him, encouraging him to finish me off. There wasn't any way I was going to let that happen. Grasping my blood-stained face in my hands and wincing with pain, I turned away from him, and without saying another word, I headed for the door. Thankfully, it wasn't as busy as it had been earlier, and I was able to get out without any crowds standing in my way.

As I stumbled out into the street I took a few seconds to get my bearings and then proceeded to stagger back to the hostel, checking over my shoulder constantly to make sure I wasn't being followed. I assumed Kelvin had been restrained by Anja, or perhaps the bar staff, as there was no one in sight.

Back at the room I went straight into the bathroom to inspect the damage to my face. He'd left me with a bruised chin, a bloody nose and a black eye, but I thought myself lucky. Kelvin had told me many stories of his army days and I knew what he was capable of. I'd got off lightly.

I cleaned myself up and fell onto my bed, exhausted and confused. My mind was somersaulting as I tried to unravel the events that had led to such an ugly scene, but somewhere, in the midst of it all, I thought of Emma. She was enough distraction for me that tiredness eventually overtook me, and I slept.

I awoke a few hours later with a headache from hell and a very sore face. My black eye would hardly open and it was hard to focus with the bright sunlight seeping through the window. It was going to be another beautiful day, but one I didn't plan on being a part of. Venturing out could have meant bumping into Kelvin, and the thought of feeling his fists again on my already tortured face was enough to keep my inside. I did go out momentarily to the little shop around the corner to get some supplies, but I was back within minutes with some bread, ham, cheese and wine; just enough to see me through the day.

Much of my time was spent in bed. I ventured out onto the balcony occasionally, wanting to feel the heat of the sun on my body, but my eye — completely swollen now — wasn't appreciating it.

It wouldn't have taken a genius to work out that my job with the brothers was officially over and as the minutes turned to hours and the afternoon sun turned into a clear and humid evening, I couldn't help but wonder if the previous night's events had been completely my fault, or whether I'd simply been in the wrong place at the wrong time. Again.

Chapter 5

CHAMPAGNE AND ROSA

A few days had passed since that painful night with Kelvin and his side-kick of an arsehole brother and I hadn't seen them since. I often replayed the events through my mind and wondered how Kelvin felt about me now the dust had settled. A few times I even pondered asking him for my job back, but I soon laughed it off. There wasn't any way in hell that was going to happen. I'd worked out that I had enough money left to enjoy Marbella for another week or so at the most, but being the eternal optimist, I figured I'd have no problem finding further work. After all, it had only taken me a day to hook up with the brothers so I was sure I could do it again. I decided not to worry about my financial situation and continued to party hard.

The brothers were popular and even though I'd fallen out of favour with them, it didn't damage my reputation as much as I'd expected. I was still meeting people with ease, even with the last remaining evidence of a black eye. My new friends all thought that Kelvin had completely overreacted so they didn't hold any hatred towards me at all. As I wandered around the streets of Marbella or even sunbathed on the beach, people came up to me and asked how I was.

The champagne flowed and most of the time I didn't even have to pay for it. I obviously couldn't afford it, but in the bars I frequented it was generously pushed upon me by my new friends, the rich socialites flaunting their wealth and competing with their counterparts. Who was I to say no? It wasn't just the champagne that came in abundance; there were drugs everywhere. I didn't use drugs every day but I did partake on a number of occasions.

I would spend all day on the beach working on a great tan then go back to my room, crash till around ten in the evening, shower, change and go out and party until sunrise, mingling with people I would never have met back in London. The majority of people I mixed with were from a completely different background. As well as the rich circle, many people I met were criminals on the run from the UK, and it did occur to me on a number of occasions that there was a much darker, seedier side to the apparent carefree lifestyle most seemed to enjoy. To be honest, I was starting to enjoy this different way of life — this darker, hedonistic side.

One particular night, with only enough money left for a couple of drinks, I decided to venture out. It was around ten that I decided to go and find a bar in a different location. I came across a quiet place; a small, typically Spanish tapas bar. It was just what I was looking for — somewhere hidden away from the main tourist areas and not too busy. There were just a handful of people dotted around, which was great. I really wasn't in the mood for conversation.

Half way through my second beer and contemplating how I was going to go about finding a job the following day, a couple came up to the bar and stood alongside me.

"Anyone sitting here?" the guy asked in a strong, Yorkshire accent, nodding his head at two empty stools.

"Nope, go ahead," I said. Please don't talk to me... please.

"Cheers mate." He picked up the cocktail menu. "I'm Peter. This is Rosa."

She was beautiful. Tall, slim, dark shoulder length hair, dark brown eyes — a classic Latin beauty. She looked around my age, in her late twenties.

"I'm Dave," I replied, staring back into my glass.

"How long have you been in Marbella?" he asked, as he tried to get the barman's attention. "Where are you staying?"

Just go away, I thought. Why all the questions? I laughed to myself, suddenly realising how the bar owner must have felt on my very first night.

"I've been here for a week or so," I said. I counted the days in my head; it seemed like so much longer than that.

"Having a good time?" He turned to look at me and before I could answer him he said: "What the hell happened to your face?"

More bloody questions.

"I'm having a great time," I told him. "The eye's fine. You should have seen the other bloke."

He laughed as I finished my beer.

"Another one?" he asked, gesturing towards my empty glass.

"Yeah sure!" I said. "A San Miguel. Cheers."

He ordered two cocktails and my beer, and I sat there hoping he wasn't expecting me to get the next round because there was no chance of that happening. The barman put the drinks on the bar with a fresh bowl of peanuts and Peter excused himself, heading off to the toilet.

"So, what really happened, Dave?" Rosa said. She had a very sexy Spanish accent but her English pronunciation was perfect.

I took a sip of my beer and looked at her. She was stunning. "I was doing a bit of work for someone when I arrived," I told her. "He thought I was trying to chat up his girlfriend so he walloped me a couple of times."

"And were you?"

"No. He was good to me. He gave me a break when I got here, so the last thing I wanted to do was to screw things up. She was a beautiful girl. Really nice, too. But she was a bit flirty that night and he got pissed off about it."

"Have you got a girlfriend?" she said, seductively playing with the cocktail straw in her mouth.

"Nope, not here anyway. I'm on my own".

"Oh right, good!" she said, smiling at me.

Peter returned from the gents. "So, what have I missed?" he asked, picking up his cocktail.

"Not much," I told him. I really didn't want any more trouble.

Peter slipped his arm around Rosa's waist, but she pulled away from him. I wondered what the score was between them but as I didn't have enough money to buy any more drinks, I knew I wouldn't find out. I finished my beer and stood up.

"Right I'm off," I said. "I was only coming out for a couple."

"Oh Dave, come on stay!" Rosa pleaded.

"I can't. I left my wallet in my room. I'm sorry!"

"It's on us. You can buy next time," she went on.

"Yeah, come on mate," Peter said. "It's fine."

"Well, as long as you're sure?" I said, sitting back down.

With another round of Champagne cocktails, we clinked glasses and moved away from the bar onto the L shaped sofas that surrounded the dance floor. Rosa sandwiched herself between Peter and myself. The bar was getting busier by the hour and the music was getting louder.

"So what's the story with you two?" I asked boldly. The alcohol was taking effect and I was beginning to lose my inhibitions.

"Just friends, aren't we?" Rosa said, looking straight at Peter.

"Yes. Just friends," he said, staring down at the terracotta tiled floor. It was obvious he wasn't happy about it.

There were a few moments of uncomfortable silence which Rosa finally broke.

"Peter... go and get some more cocktails. These are going down too quickly! Same again Dave?"

Before I could even answer her, Peter was out of his seat and heading back to the bar. As much as I was attracted to Rosa and as much as I fancied another drink, I felt bad. Back in London I'd have never been in this situation; I always paid my way. I glanced over at Peter, waiting to be served. The poor guy was besotted with her and it seemed he was willing to do anything to win her affection. As I chatted with Rosa, I watched him from the corner of my eye. At least three times he looked over his shoulder to see what we were doing.

Even though Rosa was Spanish, she'd lived in London for many years, working in P.R. She'd met Peter at a party a year before and he'd been infatuated with her ever since. Nothing had gone on between them, she told me, not even a kiss. They were friends, but that's as far as it went.

Peter returned with a different selection of cocktails this time, and they were good. Damned good. I thanked him and we clinked glasses again. I felt sorry for him and wanted to give him some of my time.

"So Peter," I said. "I detect a slight accent. Where are you from?"

"Leeds."

"A Leeds fan then?"

"Yep. Had a season ticket for twenty years. But I've been here for three now, so there's not much point in having one now. I watch them on the telly when I can."

"They've had a great year," I said. As a football fan, I knew they'd just won the league.

"Yep! I'm proud to be a Yorkshire man." He smiled for the first time in ages.

Rosa's leg was brushing against mine and I shifted in my seat. "Bet you miss watching them play," I went on, trying to ignore her.

"Yeah, sometimes, but you can't beat being here. Sun, sea and... well, you know the other one!" He looked at Rosa, his face full of expectation, but she looked away, placing her hand in the tiny space between us to discreetly stroke my thigh.

The drinks were being consumed pretty quickly and Rosa caught the barman's attention and motioned another round. The barman brought them over and as we clinked glasses again, I couldn't help but think of how stunning she looked in her tight jeans, with her white shirt a perfect contrast to her tan. The top few buttons were undone and it was hard not to notice her cleavage.

A little while later, another tray of cocktails arrived. I was losing count now. They were either on the house or I'd missed something. The alcohol was definitely taking effect.

"So Peter," I said, with a slight hint of a drunken slur, "what d'ya do here? For work, I mean." I was hoping he'd be able to help me out, point me in the right direction.

"Em. . ."

Whether he'd have given me an honest answer, I'll never know, because Rosa stood up, grabbed my hand and pulled me onto the dance floor.

She was one hot mover, her lean body moving perfectly with the beat of the music. One song led to another and we danced the night away, completely oblivious to our surroundings. Peter disappeared without us even noticing and I had a slight twinge of guilt, but it was soon forgotten. This girl wasn't taken and I'd done nothing wrong.

The hours passed by in a blur of heady, intoxicating lust. It must have been early in the morning when we eventually left because, as we were heading back to her apartment, there was a most beautiful sunrise.

It was the following afternoon when we emerged from under the sheets of her bed. She was a beautiful, sexy, passionate woman and I'd had an amazing time. I watched her, spellbound, as she plucked her silky robe from the floor, put it on and headed towards the kitchen to make us a bite to eat. She reappeared — an absolute vision — with an appetizing platter of bread, cheese and fruits, along with an iced jug of sangria to wash it down. Out on the balcony we ate, drank, talked and laughed. Peering out across the town to the ocean below, with the sun beating down on us, I felt so happy, and as I soaked in the surroundings and saw the smile on Rosa's face, I didn't have a care in the world.

Chapter 6

CHICKEN BONES

It seemed like a far and distant memory when Rosa, wearing a sexy white bikini, had blown me a kiss from her terrace as I'd left her apartment a few days before. Since our magical time together, my financial situation had deteriorated dramatically; in fact I didn't have a cent to my name. My confidence faltered and it hit me hard. Without having a clue what to do or which way to turn, my usual state of optimism quickly turned to pessimism and I plummeted to a darkness that I had never been to before. I had no job, no prospect of one and therefore no money to pay the rent, which was mounting up into a serious debt. Unable to face anyone or anything, I didn't leave my room for days. I didn't even move from my bed. To shower and shave was such an effort for me so my personal hygiene was being neglected. The rent I owed was increasing daily and I was starving, having not eaten in days. Just like back in London I'd become a recluse, but this time I didn't have the benefit of being at my parents' house with a fridge full of food and their company and support. I was in a foreign country, broke, and totally alone.

Hunger got the better of me as I rummaged through the bin next to my bed and found the unpleasant remains of some chicken pieces which had been fresh a few days before. I devoured what was left of them, even eating the insides of the bones. Swallowing my last disgusting mouthful and realising what I'd just done, I loathed myself. How the hell did I get into this fucking mess? My thoughts turned to my family and what my Mum would have thought had she known what a state I was in and how I was living. "Don't worry Mum, I'll be fine", were my last words to her as I'd left them at the airport. But I was far from fine. I thought about my night out in London and how things could have been so different had I chosen to stay at home that night. I felt sorry for myself but there was no one else to blame; the drinking, the drugs, the partying and living beyond my means had got me into this state and it was entirely my fault. I buried my face into the pillow, my head spinning with thoughts of my next move. Where was I going to go? What was I going to do? I had to focus; I needed to sort out the mess I was in. With a sudden urge to call my Mum and hear a friendly voice, I crept into the hallway of the hostel and used the public phone. Shamefully, I reversed the charges. The operator asked for the number and I held on as she put me through.

"Hello", a softly spoken voice said at the other end of the phone. It was Mum.

"Hi Mum. . . it's Dave, from sunny Spain," I replied cheerfully.

She sounded so happy to hear it was me on the other end of the line. My heart sank.

"Hi darling, it's so wonderful to hear from you. How are you?"

"I'm good Mum and having a great time. Marbella's such a nice place". I just couldn't bring myself to tell her about the state I was in. She sounded so happy.

"I was just telling Minnie and Sid that I hadn't heard from you for a few days!"

They were my parents' best friends. It must have been a Thursday night as they always hooked up at my parents place on that day, regular as clockwork. I'd lost all track of time.

"Well, here I am now! Send them my love. How is everyone?"

"They're all well, darling. They miss you, you know."

"Tell them I miss them too. Mum. I better go, this will cost you loads. I'll call you soon. I love you."

"Okay darling, keep in touch. I love you too," she said with a parting kiss down the phone.

I put the receiver down. I must have stared at it for a minute or two. I imagined Mum and Dad with their friends having a laugh and a drink, Dad sitting in HIS chair in the living room. I wished I was back there, joining in with the conversation. Dad was a Spurs fan — just like Bob and Gary — and Stuart was obsessed with Manchester United. Pink supported Chelsea, but only because she had a thing for Ray Wilkins. Sid was a Gooner — an Arsenal supporter. The conversation always ended up being about who the best team in North London was.

I went back to my room. It was around nine in the evening. Lying on my bed with my hands behind my head, I looked at the ceiling once again. I knew every single crack, crease and patch of damp on that ceiling. The conversation with Mum was the only thing I could think about. All I wanted was to be in Mum's kitchen, listening to her talk about her day whilst she made dinner for the family.

I was a twenty seven year old man but the urge to be in the home where I grew up was overwhelming. I didn't know what was happening to me. I had never felt this desperate or lonely before. I was trapped in my thoughts of home when a sharp knock at the door made me jump into consciousness.

"Open the door! I want to talk with you now! I heard you on the phone. Open the door!"

It was the owner of the hostel. Shit, this is all I fucking need, I thought. He hammered on the door and I had no choice but to answer it.

"Okay, one minute," I yelled, as I quickly hurried around the room and cleared some of the mess away. When I opened the door, he forced his way in.

"I have not seen you for days. A week. You owe money, over a week. I need it now," he demanded as he inspected the room.

"I know, I know. I'm sorry. I have no more work at the moment."

"That is not my fucking problem. You owe me money." He became a little aggressive and started waving his hands and pointing at me.

"I just spoke to my Mum back in England and she's sending me some money, so as soon as I get it I will give you what I owe you," I lied, grabbing the chicken bones from the bed and tossing them into the bin.

"Okay, but you better. I need the money. In a couple of days, yes?"

"Yes, it should be here by then. I'll pay you." It was all bullshit.

"Good. I see you in a couple of days." He opened the door and closed it behind him.

I went back to my usual position of lying on the bed and staring at the ceiling. Fuck, I was bored of it. I knew I had to do something, and fast. The landlord would be back in a couple of days for his rent so I had to find some work somehow. I needed money for food, too — I hadn't eaten in days and I was starving. My mind swam with the mess of it all and I closed my eyes. When I felt my eyelids getting heavier I was relieved, because I knew that within a few minutes I'd be oblivious to it all and miles away from the nightmare that lay ahead for me.

I woke up a few hours later with thin beams of sunlight filtering through the gaps of the window shutters, accentuating the dust that swirled around the room. I jolted out of bed and for the first time in days I turned on the shower taps to release the water. It gurgled and splattered and when it finally came to life I stood beneath it, just letting the water fall over me. After a few minutes I washed and when I felt almost human again I stepped out, dried myself off and got dressed. I was determined to find some work; any work.

Without a cent to my name, I left the hostel and made my way to the main strip of Marbella, stopping to pick a couple of oranges from the trees outside that I ate on the way.

I went to bars; I went to shops, but nothing — I couldn't speak the language which was a big problem. I avoided the bars I'd worked in with Kelvin and his brother; in fact I stayed completely away from that area, not wanting to bump into them, to face them. Rosa sprang to mind and I thought she could possibly help me, but I didn't want to ask. I may have had next to nothing, but I still had my pride — the very thing that had stopped me asking my Mum for help. It was an impossible situation. My confidence was shattered and I sank deeper into a pit of depression. For two days I searched for some work without success and all I had eaten were the oranges from the trees outside my room.

On my third uneventful day I returned to the hostel, praying that the owner wouldn't be at his desk, and I breathed a sigh of relief when I saw his empty chair. I sprinted up the two flights of stairs to my room, quickly unlocked the door, closed it behind me and turned the key. I lay on the bed, not even bothering to get undressed. Exhausted, I tried to plan my next move but I couldn't see any way out. My eye lids started to close and my body was so weak that I drifted off to sleep.

I woke up in a total panic with loud banging against the door.

"Open the fucking door now! Where's my fucking money? I want it now!"

I said nothing. I froze.

"Open the door before I fucking break it down!"

He kept shouting and banging on the door and I was scared. I scrambled out of bed and opened the windows to let some air into the room. The sun was shining. It was morning. I turned the key in the door and opened it, and he forced his way in, turning his nose up at me and pushing me to one side. He looked around in dismay; the room was in a complete state. I hurriedly dashed around, picking up my belongings from the floor and apologising profusely.

"Where's my money? You said you will have it from England, now where the fuck is it?" His face was turning red with anger.

"I'm sorry. I haven't got it. I don't know when I will have any," I said as I wiped his spit from my face.

"You fucking told me your mother will be sending some. Now where is it?" He came closer to me.

I was terrified. "I haven't got any. I'm sorry," I pleaded with him.

"You leave right now!" He pointed to the door. "Go now, fuck off!" he screamed.

Taking hold of my arm, he led me to the door. He was a big guy and I was too weak to fight back.

"You leave everything with me and when you get money, you can have it back."

"Okay, okay," I said. "Let me just put everything in my suitcase, please."

He let go of my arm and I threw all my belongings into the case and closed it. He pushed me away and grabbed the handle.

"Now fuck off and don't come back until you have the money, or this is mine."

I managed to grab my passport from the bedside table and quickly hurried out of the door, down the stairs and into the street with nothing more than the clothes on my back.

I picked another orange and wandered across the square in front of the hostel. It was a beautiful, cloudless day and the sun was blazing. Taking the first right after the tapas bar, I stepped into a small cobblestoned alley and walked through it until I came to a church. It was a pretty building — mainly white with some brown stone cladding and a spiral reaching up towards the sky. As I looked up at it, the bells began to chime. They stopped at ten. With the entire day ahead of me, I ambled through the grounds of the churchyard, kicking my feet through the lush, green lawn. The whole area was surrounded by shrubs and trees that were swaying in the cool, light breeze. There was a bench facing the entrance to the church across from the cemetery, and I walked over to it and sat down. Unless something miraculous happened, and fast, I knew there was a very real possibility I'd be sleeping there that night.

Chapter 7

THE SON OF ELVIS

The sound of the bells made me jump. Twice they rang. I'd fallen asleep on the bench facing the entrance to the church and when I woke up with the sun beating down on me, my shirt was clinging to my skin. I sat up, wiped the sleep from my eyes and tried to moisten my mouth, but my tongue felt too fat for it, my lips were cracked and I was seriously dehydrated. Remembering the fountain I'd passed on my way to the church, I decided to retrace my steps.

The small, cobblestoned square, which was closely hemmed in by Georgian style buildings, was bustling with people. I glanced across at the cafe in the corner where families and couples were sheltering under umbrellas and protecting themselves from the scorching afternoon sun. They were talking and laughing, sipping their coffee and beer, and I tried to ignore the sudden stab of envy in my chest.

The water in the fountain swirled around a carved stone basin, trickling over a handful of coins which had been tossed in by visitors. For a moment I contemplated scooping them out but they amounted to little more than a few pence at the most. I cupped the cold water in both hands, splashed my face a few times and drank until my thirst had been quenched. Standing up, I felt a little more human. I heard the church bells chime again in the distance and it struck me how strange it felt to have no time restraints or schedule. With no money or belongings and no place to call home, the town was just a vast, lonely space of possible opportunities. I could have gone anywhere, but the beach seemed like my best option.

The soft, white sand beneath my feet felt wonderful and I dug my toes in, stretching them out as I walked. Again, it was crowded and there were beautiful people in every direction I looked. I watched them for a while, noticing the smiles and care-free looks on their faces, wondering what their plans were for the afternoon and evening ahead. I turned my attention to the sea, sparkling in a magnificent blue beneath a matching cloudless sky, and having already undressed, I ran straight in. The water was cold but so refreshing, and I swam past the holiday makers who were playing and splashing until I was alone. Diving under the water felt surreal; it was so tranquil and peaceful, still and silent. My troubles seemed to leave me as I became absorbed with nothing more than my body gliding through the waves and the sea-bed below.

As I surfaced, the sound of the people on the beach magnified and I swam back towards the voices until I could stand. I waded towards the shore, walking against the strength of the tide. The waves crashed around my ankles and as each one receded it took with it some of the sand I had just been standing on. The sensation of the ground shifting beneath my feet was weird, and when I stared down at the water ebbing and flowing around me, I felt dizzy. Standing still for a moment, I attempted to get my bearings and stop my head from spinning. I knew it was the lack of food and the sudden exertion which had caused me to feel so terrible, so I slowly made my way to an empty spot on the sand, dropped my jeans and shirt in a heap and lay down. I could hear fellow sunbathers laughing and talking close by and the hissing of music coming from their headphones. A dog barked in the distance. The noises mingled together until they were nothing more than a comforting hum in my head, and before long I was asleep.

I was awoken by a wet, hot tongue licking my face. Sadly it wasn't one of the beautiful topless women who were sunbathing earlier in the day, but a puppy. I pushed it away, wiping the saliva from my face and sat up, shivering. I'd been asleep for a few hours and the sun was slowly disappearing into the horizon. The beach was near enough deserted, there were just a few stragglers packing up for the day and a handful of couples strolling hand in hand along the shore. The puppy — a black Labrador with a shiny black coat — was still beside me. It cocked its head curiously, stared at me with big, innocent eyes and promptly licked its arse. I couldn't help but laugh.

"Oh, thanks a lot!" I said."

"Hey man, sorry about that. Is the bitch being a pain in the butt?"

An eccentric looking guy — obviously American judging by his accent — towered over me. He was well over six feet tall, painfully thin with shoulder length blonde matted hair and a rather unkempt goatee. He had a joint hanging from his mouth.

"Na it's cool. I just got a tongue bashing on my face," I said jokingly, patting the pup on her head.

"Sorry dude. Come here Hound Dog!" He picked her up and stared out to sea, blowing smoke rings with the last remains of the joint.

I pushed myself up from the sand, put on my jeans, grabbed my shirt and started to make my way to the sea to wash the crap from my face.

"Hey dude, what you up to, man?" He flicked the finished joint through the air.

"Just gonna wash my face. Why"? I stopped and turned to look at him. Fuck he looked rough.

"Join me for a smoke if you want man, unless you have anything better to do?"

Anything better? I thought. Yeah, right. "Sure, thanks!" I said. "Just give me five minutes." I picked up the joint he'd discarded and put it in my pocket.

With a washed face, I joined my new American friend on an old tartan blanket, covered in dog hair. He passed me a ready rolled joint.

"Here dude. It's pretty strong weed."

"Thanks." I lit it and inhaled. "Shit, that is strong," I said, coughing a couple of times before carrying on. It didn't take long to feel the familiar sensation in my head. I'd smoked weed before, but this was something else! "This is good shit, really good," I told him, before passing it back. "So where're you from?"

"America, man. Hollywood. The place where it all happens!" He took another drag. "Here man, you finish it."

I took a couple more hits and felt relaxed for the first time in days. His pup was resting her head on my leg with her body on the blanket next to me. "How long have you been here?" I asked him, glancing up and down the beach. The place was deserted.

"Three months dude, sleeping right here on the sand. Just me and the bitch. Been travelling around Spain, hanging out, getting high and enjoying life, man!" He started to roll another joint. "What about you? What's your story?"

I told him about London and what had happened with the brothers. They seemed a distant memory now. I told him about getting kicked out of the hostel and meeting Rosa and Emma.

"You lucky bastard! You've been here only a couple of weeks and fucked a couple of chicks? Man, I'm jealous. Good going!" He lit the joint and then suddenly raised his head in excitement. "Hey Dude, stay here! Crash here tonight, on the beach. You know, on the blanket!"

Why not? I thought. I've got nowhere else to go. "Cool!" I said. "Sounds good to me!"

We had a few more joints. I was so wasted. We talked shit as I lay on the blanket, listening to the waves crashing in the distance and staring at the stars scattered across the dark, night sky. The moon was glowing in its full glory, lighting up the sea below. It looked amazing.

"So man, what's ya name?" He'd manoeuvred his body from an upright position and was lying on the blanket beside me with Hound Dog sandwiched between us.

"At the moment it could be anything," I replied, "but normally it's Dave. Yours?"

"No name," he said, quite seriously. He looked at me, his eyes bloodshot. "They call me the Son of Elvis." He smirked and stretched his arms out towards the sky.

"The son of Elvis?" I repeated as I nearly choked on the smoke I'd just inhaled.

"Yeah, man. My old man was Elvis. Elvis fucking Presley. Rock n Roll King of the fucking world. He was never around. Hardly saw him. But when I did, he called me the Son of Elvis." He paused, as if he was trying to capture a long lost memory. "No name, nothing," he went on. "Fucking nothing."

I went along with him. He was just wasted; he'd been living rough too long and was fucked up on drugs.

Over the next few hours we were completely under the influence of the weed and rambled incoherently. The pup, Hound Dog, was gently snoring and practically lying on top of me, but I had no complaints. The cold air had started to drift in from the sea and she was keeping me warm. The Son of Elvis was totally wrecked and just staring at the stars, dribbling from his mouth. I felt compassion for him; he was one mixed up guy.

It was around six in the morning, I guess, when the man with no name suddenly woke up, stood and started to search for his rucksack. "Food! Where's the fucking food?"

I'd been awake for a few minutes — having been woken up by the pup again, licking my face like it was her arse — but long enough to know I was starving.

"Dude, you wanna eat?" He unzipped a section of the rack sack and took out some bread and ham.

"Sure, can you spare it?"

"I wouldn't have asked, man."

I watched him take out two slices of white bread and a couple of slices of ham. He placed the ham on one piece and closed the sandwich with both hands. As he'd been sleeping rough, his hands were covered in filth and his fingernails were black. I hesitated for a split second, but hunger prevailed. "Thanks," I told him. And I meant it.

I took my time eating it, aware that this may have been the last bit of food I'd get for a while. I could have had another, but I didn't want to take advantage of his kindness.

We talked further as the sun peeked over the ocean and started to warm the air. He rolled another joint and we smoked it. I wandered where he got his weed from, but didn't want to ask.

"So man," he said, "what're your plans today?"

"Have a swim, search for work and see what happens, I guess."

"Good plan dude, good plan," he muttered as he lay back down on the blanket and closed his eyes.

I watched him for a while, his chest rising and falling in an easy rhythm. The guy would be asleep before long.

"Hey" I said. "I'm gonna get going now. Perhaps I'll see you around? And thanks for the smoke and everything. It was good to meet you." I got up from the blanket rather unsteadily. "See ya, Hound Dog" I whispered, patting her head.

"Sure, cool man, see ya soon." His eyes were closed and he was singing to himself. All I made out as I walked away was that it was an Elvis song.

Considering I'd slept on the beach I felt pretty good, but I needed to clear my head. I looked around and as there was no one in sight I stripped off and ran into the sea. "Jesus!" I shouted as the water washed over me. Although it was freezing, it was invigorating.

I spent most of the day walking around the town looking for work, but who was going to offer a job to a homeless man with an unkempt appearance? I watched with envy people eating in cafés, drinking in bars, laughing and having fun. The day slowly passed into night and the streets became lit by the colourful neon signs of the restaurants. As I walked the pavements I became fascinated with the people. Tourists were studying outdoor menus and being heckled by waiters to come inside. "Nice food! Good value! Much drink!" was their pitch. In some cases it worked, but mostly the waiters were ignored and people moved on to study another menu close by.

At around midnight, with families and the older couples long since departed, the restaurants closed and the streets were taken over by pretty young girls wearing shorts and miniskirts. I watched them giggling with the promoters, accepting the vouchers for their free drinks. "Come here! Great bar! It's ladies night! Buy one get one free!" It was the same old bullshit, and for a moment I wondered why I'd even taken the brothers up on their offer of work doing exactly the same thing.

I moved away from the crowds. It had been a long, hot day and I hadn't eaten since early morning. My walking had slowed to a gentle pace some hours before, but the tiredness suddenly hit me with a vengeance. I contemplated the beach again and perhaps tracking down the Son of Elvis, but common sense won through. Even if I had found him, I wasn't sure I could cope with another night on the sand and a belly full of drugs.

As I turned a corner, I came across a brightly lit and rather swish hotel. It reminded me of the one I'd stayed at on my very first night and I wanted nothing more than to turn the clock back and start again. That first night in Marbella was amazing; the room and balcony, the power shower, the crisp and clean bed sheets. And how could I ever forget Emma, straddling me and making love to me. I was so glad she couldn't see me then.

Without thinking too clearly and to get away from the busy streets, I wandered into the hotel lobby. To my surprise I found it empty — there wasn't a soul to be seen. Even the reception desk was deserted. A bit further in, to the left, I spotted a black leather sofa and I headed towards it. My initial intention had been to sit for a while, away from the noise on the streets, and rest my feet. But it wasn't long before I lowered my tired body onto the soft leather. I stretched out, glancing around at the artwork adorning the walls and then curled up on my side. My eyes were heavy, dragging themselves closed, and within seconds I drifted into a very deep sleep.

Chapter 8

A RUDE AWAKENING

Semi-conscious and disorientated, I sensed a presence, someone standing over me. But rubbing my eyes, all I could see was a blur of multi-coloured geometric shapes all interlocked and swirling around. Even before I had time to register what was going on, I felt my body being held down against my will. There was a tight, heavy feeling in my throat, I struggled to breathe and I couldn't move. Was I dreaming? Was I having a moment of sleep paralysis?

Was I fuck!

As soon as I opened my eyes I realised that I'd been temporarily blinded by the early morning sun that was glaring through the leaded windows across the foyer, but more alarmingly, I made out the huge pair of hands that had grabbed hold of my shirt collar. In a panic I tried to get away, but I was suddenly lifted from the sofa and dragged the entire length of the foyer with my feet barely touching the white marbled floor. I managed to lift my head to glance around for any signs of help, but the place was deserted. The man holding me hastened his step and it felt like I was on a train, with the pictures on the walls flashing past me at an incredible speed. When he started yelling in my face, I jerked my head away to escape his rancid breath. He smelt of alcohol and cigarettes and appeared to be quite intoxicated as he grumbled through his nicotine-stained handlebar moustache.

He dragged me towards the hotel exit, contorting one of my arms into a completely unnatural position behind my back. I yelled: "let go of me, you bastard!" but he ignored me. I tried to manoeuvre my way out of his grip but it was impossible; he was over six feet tall and built like a tank. His shaven head, intense bloodshot eyes and thick solid neck loomed ominously out of his short sleeved uniformed shirt. He continued his verbal assault towards me, every syllable of his tirade teeming with rage, and even though I couldn't understand what he was saying I knew that he wasn't inviting me for breakfast. My head pounded from the shock and his voice vibrated right through to my bones. Then in one motion, and still shouting ferociously, he kicked opened the double glass panelled doors and physically threw me out of the building.

I fell awkwardly onto the hard concrete ground and it knocked the breath from my lungs, winding me. Just a few feet away from my painful landing were the well-trimmed, soft lush gardens of the hotel. Why the hell couldn't I have landed there? With his thick tattooed arms flailing, he started shooing me away like a stray dog, and just in case I hadn't got the message, he planted one of his boots into my rib-cage. I reeled in pain as I crawled away, snatching back my passport which had fallen from my pocket. He approached me again, but when a young Spanish couple who had been sitting on a nearby bench stood up and walked towards me, he backed off and disappeared inside. With their help, I managed to pull myself up, clutching my side where the bastard had kicked me. I thanked them, assuring them that I was ok and staggered away, passing restaurants and bars and holding onto their railings and menu stands for support. The flashing neon light displays of the previous night were now just a lifeless traffic of florescent tubes entwined with wires and cables. There was no sign of life anywhere; the place was like a ghost town.

Slowly, I made my way to the beach. It was deserted apart from a handful of joggers out for an early morning run and a few old-timers enjoying the quiet time before the onslaught of tourists would emerge. The sand was soft, but felt damp and uninviting from the morning dew. I slumped onto it, pulling my legs towards my chest, my ribs throbbing with every move and jolt. Looking around, I spotted Chico's in the distance, the bar where I'd met Kelvin and his brother on my second day. It seemed like a lifetime ago. Back then I'd felt young and free, looking at the world through expectant eyes, but right then I felt as old as the trees. I scanned the beach, looking for The Son of Elvis, my American friend. A friendly face, a shoulder to lean on and a much needed hit of a strong joint to sooth the pain would have been wonderful, but I couldn't see him or Hound Dog anywhere.

I sat staring out to sea and felt the soft ocean breeze drift towards me. The sea was a beautiful colour but I couldn't identify it. Was it aquamarine? I counted the waves, each one becoming stronger, and watched the seventh one crash against the shore. The golden rays of sun burned through the last remaining white cloud in the sky and it was such a welcome feeling that I uncurled myself and stretched out on the sand. My ribs throbbed but I lay there waiting for the sun to work its magic and heal me. A little while later, and somewhat soothed, I shed my clothes, placed them on the sand and bathed in the sea for as long as I could manage.

I emerged feeling cleansed and sunk into the warmth and softness of the sand. Closing my eyes, my thoughts turned to my family, and a tear trickled from the corner of my eye. I was lonely, tired and in pain and would have given anything to magic myself back home — to have Mum fussing around me, making me tea and toast. I had neither money nor food, my belongings were out of reach and I had no return ticket to the UK. In fact my only possessions were my passport and the clothes on my back.

I must have fallen asleep for some time because when I awoke, it was to the gentle hum of conversation, and I found myself surrounded by holiday makers unpacking their bags, stripping off their clothes and laying their towels on the sand. The muted hues of the desolate beach a few hours earlier had transformed into a blur of colour and I lay there for a while, my eyes picking out the greens, oranges and pinks of swimwear. There was a blonde nearby rubbing oil into her skin and I watched her, mesmerised, as she rubbed and massaged it up and down the length of her legs. She was amazingly toned and had I been a photographer, I'd have positioned her in the exact spot she was standing in — with the sun to her side, highlighting the small dragon tattoo on her inner left thigh. When she removed her bikini top and produced a pair of beautiful, natural breasts that bounced every time she moved, I couldn't help but feel aroused. I shifted on to my side to make it a little less obvious, but I carried on watching her. Being discreet had never been one of my strong points, and when she started to oil up her breasts, it was obvious that she was doing it for her audience. She seductively rubbed them — her left, then her right — and then, as if to rub it in even more, she tweaked her nipples. For a moment I actually believed I was in with a chance — and that just intensified the stirring in my boxer shorts — but it was short-lived. Her equally beautiful boyfriend appeared, took hold of the oil and began massaging it into her back. I turned away at that point, thinking about what a lucky bastard he was, and as my erection subsided I wondered if I'd get the opportunity to meet someone of my own. As much as I tried to put her out of my mind, I couldn't help but think of Rosa.

Bored with the beach, I decided to leave the beautiful couple to it and take a walk into the main town of Marbella. The streets were busy with tourists searching for gifts to take back to loved ones and the cafés were full of people having a late breakfast or an early lunch. As the smell of fried bacon and freshly brewed coffee wafted through the air, I tried to ignore my hunger and wandered aimlessly around the town wondering where my next meal would come from and where I'd be sleeping that night.

It was some time later, turning the corner from a side road onto the main street, that I was unexpectedly distracted and a familiar face caught my eye. I'm not a religious man but at that very moment I did wonder if God was on my side. It was Rosa, looking as gorgeous as ever in a pair of black shorts and a white shirt. I'd only been thinking of her a few hours before and I couldn't believe my luck. She saw me

and waved, and I waved back — undoubtedly grinning like an idiot.
As she made her way towards me with the mid-morning sunlight
dappling her skin, she looked so fresh faced and beautiful, and for a
split second I wanted to run towards her, take her in my arms and
plant a kiss on her lips. But catching a glimpse of my reflection in
a shop window, I stopped abruptly. Shit, I looked a mess. My face
was haggard and unshaven, my eyes were weary and my once white
shirt — now with a ripped collar — was badly in need of a wash. As
Rosa got closer, I quickly brushed my fingers through my hair, my
grin diminishing to a half smile, and then suddenly she was in front
of me, leaning in to kiss my cheek. She smelt beautiful and I cringed
and blushed, knowing how I looked.

"Dave! How are you? It's so good to see you!"

"Hey, Rosa!" I said, dying on the inside. "I'm good thanks, how are
you?" It wouldn't have taken a genius to see that I was on my knees
and I wondered if she was just being polite by completely ignoring
my appearance.

"I'm great!" She raised her head towards the sky, her state of the
art sunglasses protecting her eyes from the strong glare of the sun.
"Beautiful day, isn't it?"

We chatted a little awkwardly at first, mostly due to my embarrass-
ment, but after a few minutes our conversation became more relaxed
and to my complete surprise she actually started to flirt with me.
The innuendoes were flying back and forth and for a while I actually
forgot the state I was in.

"It's my best friend's birthday today," she told me. "There's a party
tonight, on the Marina. I'd love you to come! There'll be plenty of
food and drink!"

And then it was back: reality hitting me full in the face. I shook my
head, convinced she was inviting me out of pity. As much as I longed
to spend some time with her and get some food in my stomach, my
pride was still intact and that was pretty much all I had left.

"Oh come on Dave," she pleaded, "it'll be fun! Look, come back
to my apartment, have a siesta and a shower and then we can go to

the party together. Deal?"

As stupid as it sounds, I did actually consider refusing, but when she untied her ponytail, tossed her hair across her shoulders and gave me the most beautiful smile, it didn't take long for me to change my mind. Maybe there is a God? I thought to myself.

My confidence grew with every step as we strolled hand in hand through the streets of Marbella to her apartment. Rosa didn't once mention how I looked, but when we arrived, I immediately took up her offer of a much needed shower. The sea had been refreshing, but there was no substitute for hot water and soap and I stayed there for as long as I thought I could get away with. Rosa stepped into the shower after me and I lay on her bed, listening to the trickle of the water, waiting for her to join me. I must have nodded off briefly, because the next minute she was kneeling on the bed wrapped in nothing but a towel and softly kissing my lips. I sleepily kissed her back, pulling her towards me, and when she let the towel fall from her body, I tossed it onto the floor. I was aroused instantly and within seconds I was inside her, moaning against her lips. We made love, fast and frenzied, with Rosa's wet hair falling across my face and her nails digging into my back with each thrust of my body. I fucked her until I knew she was close, and when she threw her head back and opened her mouth wide in a silent scream, I came too, feeling a week's worth of tension leave me.

Once we managed to force ourselves away from the bedroom, we lounged on the terrace and indulged in a delicious tray of tapas. Rosa had prepared a jug of iced Sangria too, and I feasted on it all, trying not to appear too greedy. The scene was perfect — so romantic — and besides Rosa looking astonishingly beautiful, the sky was as colourful as a rainbow as the sun slowly receded into the ocean. The conversation between us flowed so easily and with each passing moment I liked her even more. What had started off as an unexpected encounter was rapidly turning into something more and I couldn't wait to spend the evening with her, laughing and partying the night away, before slipping back into bed.

When the sun had said its farewell and the breeze had reached us from the ocean, we headed back inside. Rosa had kindly washed my clothes and I dressed quickly before perching on the end of the bed to watch her get ready. Seeing her put her clothes on was just as erotic as seeing her take them off, and I fought the desire to make love to her all over again.

In hindsight, I wish I had. In fact in hindsight, I should never have stepped out the door.

Chapter 9

THE PARTY

The elevator came to a halt on the ground floor and the doors slid open. As we passed the reception desk in the hallway, the old man sitting behind it looked over the glasses perched on the end of his nose and acknowledged Rosa with a kindly smile. She waved at him, smiling back, and for a split second I remembered the bastard who still had my belongings. The two men couldn't have been more different if they'd tried, but strangely, I didn't feel angry. There was something about being with Rosa that paled everything else into insignificance.

We made our way out of the building and strolled hand in hand down the narrow, cobble-stoned lane, chatting as we went, but when we turned left onto the main street Rosa stopped in her tracks.

"What is it?" I said, watching her. Her face was lit up and she looked almost angelic, staring out into the night.

"I've always loved the Marina," she said, "ever since I was a little girl. It's just so sparkly and pretty."

I smiled, wrapping my arm around her and pulling her close, and we stood quietly for a while, watching the flickering lights from the yachts reflecting in the water. Rosa looked beautiful that night, her stunning black dress accentuating every curve of her body. Her hair was loose, flowing freely around her shoulders, and when a cool breeze caught it and blew it across her face, I softly swept it away.

"Baby, I feel like the luckiest man in the world to be with you," I said, cupping her face in my hands, and I meant every word. I leaned in to kiss her and she responded, closing her eyes. I lost myself in the moment, my hands caressing her body through the silky material of her dress, and she pushed herself gently against me, her hand grasping the back of my hair. When our lips finally parted and I looked into her eyes, they were damp with tears.

"What's wrong, baby?"

"Nothing," she said, blinking them back. "It was just such a beautiful thing to say."

I kissed Rosa again, lightly on her lips, but she pulled away, giggling. Following her gaze and glancing over my shoulder, I saw that we'd gathered quite an audience! I took hold of her hand.

"C'mon, let's go," I said. "Claire will be waiting."

The Marina was only a short distance away. We turned left along the promenade and left again, and Rosa pointed out that the steps to Alameda Park.

"We must go there," she said, squeezing my fingers in her hand. "It's beautiful. There are some sculptures in the gardens. Salvador Dali. Do you know him?"

I'd had many a Dali poster adorning my walls as a teenager. "Yes, I do," I told her. "I'd love to visit."

"Then perhaps we should do that tomorrow," she said, smiling.

Tomorrow, I thought. She's planning for tomorrow. My heart swelled.

Chrome covered yachts of all sizes filled the harbour, rocking simultaneously side by side to the lapping of the waves. Muscle-bound men and gold skinned girls danced on the decks without a care in the world, and the music — a variety of rock, pop and soul — pounded out from each boat along the bay as we passed them. It was easy to see why it was labelled the playground for princes; the money in the air was evident.

We strolled along the limestone pavement weaving our way through the groups of tourists who had filled the Marina and passed a whole host of bistros, restaurants and champagne bars — each one looking more inviting than the last. When we reached the end of the strip, there, standing outside the glitzy bar where her party was being held, was Claire, smoking a cigarette.

"Wow, you look amazing", Rosa told the birthday girl as she kissed her on both cheeks. And she did. Claire was slim, blonde, and had the most amazing wide blue eyes. She looked every part the millionaire's mistress in her striking red suit, and had Rosa not told me before that Claire was single and worked as a holiday receptionist, it wouldn't have surprised me in the slightest had one of the yachts belonged to her lover.

"Claire, this is Dave, the guy I told you about."

She's mentioned me?

Claire reached out and touched my arm." So you're Dave!" she purred. "I've heard so much about you!"

"All good, I hope," I said, kissing her cheek.

"I'll tell you all about it when Rosa's not around!"

All three of us laughed and it broke the ice.

"So, how many years young are you?" I asked rather cheekily.

"Dave," Rosa interrupted, nudging me with her elbow. "You never ask a woman their age!"

I flinched — my ribs still not fully recovered from their kicking — and the smile left Rosa's face almost immediately.

"I'm sorry, babe," she said, reaching out to stroke my side.

I had no idea how much Claire knew about my recent shenanigans, but she didn't let on.

"Well, if you really want to know, I'm a quarter of a century old. Yep, I'll be twenty five in..." she glanced down at her watch and arched an eyebrow as if trying to work it out "... umm, in about fifty minutes time."

"You don't look a day over twenty-one!" I said with a wink, holding the bar door open for the girls.

The atmosphere inside was relaxed but it was getting busier by the minute. There was such an interesting mix of people and nationalities there that even The Son of Elvis wouldn't have been out of place had he arrived showered, without his dog. On the opposite end of the spectrum were the pijos who, Rosa explained, were the Spanish equivalent of a yuppy. And then there were all the people in-between, Rosa and I included.

Claire beckoned to the waiter and he arrived promptly with a silver tray balanced perfectly on the tips of his fingers.

"Here! Have some champagne!" Claire took two flutes from the tray and handed them to us as the waiter stood by, waiting to be dismissed. She thanked him and he weaved his way back through the crowds.

"Thanks!" Rosa said, raising her glass. "I have a feeling this is going to be a very good night!"

"Happy Birthday!" I said, clinking glasses with Claire. I had to agree with Rosa — we were all set to have a fantastic time.

We chatted over the music — soft, rhythmic Jazz being played by a smart three piece band that looked every bit the part in their pristine tuxedos. Two young, handsome barmen were busy showing off their skills, tossing cocktail mixers and glasses behind their backs with one hand and catching them with the other, whilst a bunch of pretty girls were admiring them and giggling to each other. The men were playing up to it, thrusting their hips and flirting outrageously.

"Who the hell do they think they are?" I whispered to Rosa. "Tom Cruise?"

She laughed and kissed me on the cheek. I have to admit though, they were pretty damn impressive.

Half an hour later the place was rammed. The guys behind the long glass top bar were in full flow — taking orders, flinging glasses and mixing an array of amazing looking cocktails. People were lounging in the corners, relaxing and chatting, while others stood and mingled, their bodies swaying to the beat of the music. Others had poured out onto the street and couples were dancing on the pavement outside, backlit by the marina lights. I watched them for a while through the huge feature window at the front of the bar and spotted a guy

who I'd met once when I was with Kelvin. He was perched on a
bench in a world of his own with an unlit cigarette stuck to his lips.
I contemplated going to say hello, but thought better of it. This was
my time with Rosa, but more importantly, I had no reason to get
involved in that scene again. It had been a mistake from the start.

"Hey guys, I'm starving. Shall we eat?" Claire piped up.

"Good idea!" I said.

We placed our empty glasses on the waiter's tray, took another
full one each and made our way to the back of the bar towards the
buffet. The tables looked incredible; they were bursting with food —
all typically Spanish — and we piled our plates with the delicious
snacks, appetizers and portions of specially made dishes which were
there for the taking. With our plates full, we headed upstairs to the
terrace which overlooked the bay and we ate in silence, taking in
the spectacular view of the moonlight stretching across the water.
Again, I looked at Rosa who was mesmerised by the twinkling lights
of the yachts moored in the bay. As I sat there eating and watching
her, I felt a shift inside of me. Admittedly, I was relieved that I had
someone on my side and that my days of sleeping on the beach were
perhaps over. But it was more than that. I really liked her. There
was a connection, an understanding, and I knew she felt it too. It
wasn't just about the physical attraction; we'd spent a lot of time
talking and it felt like we were actually going somewhere. I looked
at the people dancing and singing on the yachts in the bay, having
the time of their lives, and I smiled to myself. Right at that moment,
I felt luckier than them.

"Where's the birthday girl?" yelled the party guests downstairs.
Claire glanced at her watch and shrieked.

"It's quarter past eleven!" she said. "It's my birthday!" She hurriedly put her plate on the floor grabbing a skewered olive for the
journey, and made her way back down the stairs and into the bar.
We followed her, and as if by magic the band came to life with their
Jazz-infused version of Happy Birthday — saxophone and all. Claire's
friends sang and danced around her and she blushed as a waiter

brought out a beautiful cake with twenty five candles, each flame
flickering in the air. She pushed her hair behind each ears, lowered
her head and blew out the candles to a chorus of hip, hip hooray!

"Speech! Speech!" the guests cried.

Claire looked at us nervously but Rosa winked at her.

"Go on... you'll be fine!" she said, pushing her towards the stage.

Claire took the mic and looked out at her throng of guests.

"Okay, umm..." she stuttered, "I'd just like to say thanks for com-
ing tonight. I hope you're all enjoying yourselves and... ummm..."
She scanned the room, lost for words, and then screamed: "LET'S
PARTY!"

Her audience clapped and cheered as Claire left the stage and right
on cue the resident DJ started his gig with Happy Birthday by Stevie
Wonder. Claire was swept onto the dance floor by her friends and
within seconds it was completely full. I couldn't help but feel happy
for her — it was her night and she was loving it.

Perhaps an hour or so later, engrossed in a conversation with another couple, a tap on the shoulder was enough to make Rosa jump.
It was a rather red faced and sweaty Claire, who had been on the
dance floor for the entire time.

"Hey guys," she said. "I don't want to worry you, but guess who's
just walked in?" She nodded in the direction of the bar.

It was Peter, the friend Rosa had been with on the first night I'd
met her.

"Oh God," Rosa said. "Who invited him?"

"Not me," Claire told her, shaking her head.

Claire knew all about Peter and his incessant attempts at turning
his friendship with Rosa into something more. Having him at the
party was the last thing Claire wanted and she looked worried.

"It'll be fine," Rosa said. "We'll deal with it. Go and enjoy yourself."

As Claire made her way back onto the dance floor, Peter moved
away from the bar and headed towards us.

"Shit, look at him," I said. "He's completely pissed."

Peter staggered through the crowds, bumped into a couple on the dance floor and managed to spill half of his drink over himself. He'd obviously dressed to impress with his shirt buttons undone to the waist, but he looked like an idiot with a wet patch the size of a dinner plate down his front.

"Rosa! The beautiful Rosa," he said, with his arms outstretched and his drink sloshing precariously in his glass. "How are you, my baby?"

He was obviously expecting a hug but Rosa didn't reciprocate. Then he noticed me.

"Oh. I didn't see YOU there," he slurred. "Tell me, what was your name again?" He rubbed his chin, as if thinking about it. "Oh yeah. . . the black eyed boy!"

"Peter, do yourself a favour and leave okay?" I said, shaking my head, as Rosa stood up and made her way to my side of the table. "Look at the state of you."

Rosa slid into the chair next to mine and the couple we had been talking to stood up and left.

"Do ME a favour," Peter said, "and fuck off. I'm not leaving. It's a free country and I can do what the fuck I want." He laughed, swaying on his feet and looked around the room. "Nice party," he went on. "Where's the birthday girl?"

"She's outside having a cigarette" Rosa said bluntly.

Peter turned to me, his face contorted in anger. "So, you wanker," he spat. "What are you doing here?" His bloodshot eyes looked straight into mine with an intensity that burned right through me. For a second I thought he was going to lurch at me but when he lifted his glass and realised it was empty, he turned his attention to the waiter. He was clicking his fingers with one hand — trying to summon him over — and haphazardly wiping down his shirt with the other.

"Look mate, don't you think you've have enough?"

He raised his voice." I'm NOT your bloody mate. Don't you dare tell me what I can or can't have. You're fucking lucky I haven't come over there and blacked your other eye, you bastard."

"Hey," Rosa said. "Don't talk to Dave like that. He's done nothing wrong." She spoke to him calmly and politely with far more restraint than I could have mustered.

"I can talk however I like, Rosa. This has nothing to do with you." He was trying to stand up but only managed to embarrass himself further by falling back down onto the sofa. "I love you Rosa," he went on, "and everything was great, and then HE came along and took you away from me."

"Peter," Rosa said, "we were never together. Never. You know that. We're good friends but nothing else. Please," she pleaded, "let's keep it that way."

Peter stared into his lap with his shoulders hunched over and his head bobbing from side to side. I wasn't sure if he'd admitted defeat or was working on his next line. I leant over to whisper in Rosa's ear.

"Look, I'm gonna go for a walk okay? He's drunk and I don't want any trouble. I'll be back in an hour or so."

"You don't have to leave because of him, Dave," she said.

"I know, sweetheart. But he'll be fine once I've gone. You can chat to him, you know, let him cool off, okay?" I finished the last of my drink.

She sighed and leaned in to kiss me.

"I won't be long," I told her, "I promise. And when I get back we can go to your place."

Rosa nodded her head and gave me a half smile.

"Don't be long, baby," she said, and kissed me again.

Out on the Marina, Claire was getting some air and finishing a cigarette.

"Where are you going?" she said. "Is everything alright?"

"Everything's fine," I told her. "I'm just taking a breather, letting things calm down in there. Keep an eye on Rosa for me, will you?"

"Sure," she said, and took a final drag before crushing the cigarette in the ashtray on the table. "But don't be long, eh?"

I smiled and headed up the street with two large bottles of San Miguel for company. It was just after two and the Marina was still full of people, chatting, drinking and having fun. Smoke filled the pocket of air immediately in front of me and I lifted my head and breathed in. Ah, that sweet smell of Marijuana. I glanced to the yacht on my left and saw a group of people sitting in a circle on the deck, rolling and passing joints. Waiters to my right were busy clearing tables as the last of their diners were preparing to leave. The bars were still packed, and people were spilling out onto the streets dancing and laughing. For them, the night was far from over; they'd be partying till sunrise.

I strolled along the pavement and out of the Marina, and then turned left onto the main road. It was a clear, humid night and the stars were twinkling brightly with the full moon shining down on me. It was nice to get away from the noise and bustle of the crowds, and before long, all I could hear was the relaxing sound of chirping crickets coming from the bushes adjacent to the road. Every step I took was accompanied by a swig of beer, each one calming me down and giving me some perspective. As much as Peter was an annoying bastard, I knew he was just drunk and that in the morning he'd probably be regretting being such an asshole. I carried on walking, lost in my thoughts, until the soothing sound of the crickets was shattered by the distinctive sound of sirens in the distance. Curiously, I looked around, and in amongst the trees and hotel rooftops, I saw smoke billowing into the sky. With one last sip, I finished my beer, threw the empty bottle into a rubbish bin and unscrewed my second bottle. I took a mouthful and without any hesitation, I made my way to investigate where it was coming from.

In a couple of hours or so it would become a move that turned out to be the biggest mistake of my life.

Chapter 10

THIRTY FEET

Wailing sirens echoed down the street. Almost instantly, a procession of ambulances and police cars sped past me, their whirring lights bouncing off the hedgerows. A thick, black plume of smoke engulfed half of the sky, and with every stride I took it swallowed even more of it. Closer to the horizon, the reds, oranges and yellows of the blaze illuminated the rooftops as flames snaked towards them. Without even thinking, I finished my beer, tossed the empty bottle into the hedge and started to run. My ribs throbbed as each foot hit the pavement and when I turned a corner in the road, a sharp pain shot straight across my chest. I stumbled and fell, grazing my knees, but that was the least of my worries. "Shit!" I said out loud, clutching my side and trying to breathe. I pulled myself up, leant against the hedge and tried to supress the agony. When I looked up, my mouth fell open as I took in the sight ahead of me. A cold shiver passed over my skin and ran right through to my bones as the hairs on the back of my neck stood tall.

The fire in the building was rampant, with billowing smoke bulging from the windows. Pockets of flames swept through the ground floor as more smoke belched into the night. Firemen were on their knees, frantically trying to contain the flames that were spreading along the interior walls and bursting through the upper windows of the hotel.

The police were struggling to hold back the crowds of locals, tourists, journalists and TV reporters who were pushing forward in disbelief, some of them crying hysterically and trying to reach their loved ones. More fire-fighters, fully equipped with gas masks and oxygen tanks, made their way to the entrance, passing guests lying on the grass in their bed clothes. Some emerged distraught — crying and screaming. Others were covered in blood and gasping for air.

I stared, completely aghast, at the chaos before me, and when the flames suddenly swept across the entire ground floor of the building, I stepped back, making my way to the side of the hotel. I was in a daze, not able to take it all in, and the wailing of the sirens along with the desperate screams of people panicking filled my head. Up until then I was under the illusion that fire merely crackled, but I couldn't have been more wrong. The sounds of cracking wood, melting metal and the shattering of windows as the flames consumed whatever was in its path, was unbearable. I rambled further away from the noise, away from the devastation, and slumped against a tree. Amidst the screams from the crowd were the faint cries of people who were still in the building, begging to be helped. My stomach turned and I started to retch, the surging bile doubling me over.

"Help me!"

Desperate to block it out, I stumbled further away, but the voice just intensified. It was a woman — I could hear her now — and she was frantic.

"Please somebody help me!"

I turned to my left, then to my right, squinting my eyes to see through the dark. Then there it was again, her voice bellowing through the night.

"HELP ME!"

I looked up, seeing nothing at first, but then spotted the silhouette of a woman leaning over the railings of her balcony, trying to escape the smoke that was curling towards her. I held my hand above my eyes to focus.

"MY ROOM'S ON FIRE! HELP ME, PLEASE!" she screamed at the top of her voice.

She was alone, and nobody — fucking nobody — seemed to be heading in her direction or was even aware of her. The fact that I'd been drinking champagne and cocktails all night didn't even cross my mind. Nor did the fact that I was about to risk my life. The only thing that entered my head was getting her out of there. It was that simple.

I clasped my hands around my mouth and shouted up at her.

"Hold on! I'm coming to get you! Just stay calm okay?"

A seven foot wall which wrapped around the perimeter of the hotel stood between us, and I jumped, managing to grip the top of it with my left hand. Struggling painfully, I inched and heaved myself upwards, digging my feet into crevices in the brickwork. I stretched my other arm onto the top, hauled myself over and dropped to the ground on the other side. There was a black drainpipe running the entire height of the hotel wall alongside her balcony and I managed to pull myself onto it, gripping the rough, rusty metal as firmly as I could. I could feel the intensity of the fire on the other side, and as I climbed, my hands began to sweat. Smoke rolled from most of the rooms around me but I carried on, my eyes watering and my mouth getting dryer by the second. About two-thirds of the way up my left hand slipped, but I managed to hold on with my right, wrapping my feet tightly around the drainpipe.

"Hurry, please!" she pleaded.

"I am, I am!" I told her. "Just hold on." I may have sounded calm, but underneath I was petrified. As I pulled myself level with her, she reached out as far as she could, but we were still about two feet apart. Thick smoke was gushing through the doors from the room behind her and I knew I had to act fast. The fact that I was thirty feet off the ground and clinging on to a drainpipe didn't even occur to me and I swung my body, feet first, towards the ledge of the balcony floor.

"Shit," I said, missing it.

She was coughing and spluttering and her face was worn with fear as tears streamed down her face. With time against me, I swung again, and this time my feet connected with the ledge.

"Quick, give me your hand," I shouted. She leant over the balcony, stretching her arm towards me as far as she could, and I grabbed her, still holding onto the drainpipe. With sweat pouring off me, I counted out loud: "one... two... three", and let go of the drainpipe. She pulled me towards her and I grabbed the balcony rail with my fingertips, pulling myself onto it. I tried to calm her down — she was hysterical — but the flames were minutes away from engulfing us both.

"It's okay," I said. "I've got you. But we need to get out of here".

The flames were getting closer and the heat and smoke was unbearable.

"Look," I said. "Just do what I say, okay?"

She nodded her head, her face smudged with tears and smoke.

I climbed over the balcony rail and stood on the ledge.

"Okay, get on my back, NOW."

Thankfully she was small — only about five feet tall — and weighed next to nothing. She climbed over the rail and onto my back, wrapping her legs around my waist and her arms firmly around my neck. With my right hand gripping the balcony rail I leaned and stretched as far as I could and managed to grab the drainpipe with my left hand, balancing my foot on one of the wall brackets. I looked down. There I was, holding onto a balcony and a drainpipe with a woman on my back, thirty feet from safety with a raging fire just a stone's throw away. If only Rosa could see me now, I thought.

"Shit, Rosa!" I said out loud. What the fuck was I doing?

"Hold on tight," I told her, "and don't let go!" I took a deep breath and with as much strength as I could muster, I let go of the rail and pushed myself towards the drainpipe. When we thumped against the wall, she tightened her grip around me.

"You okay?" I asked, barely able to talk.

"Yes," she muffled, with her wet face buried deep into my neck.

Each step down was accompanied by a slip as we descended the drainpipe, which was now hanging precariously off the wall. Nearing the bottom I lost my grip, and we fell the last couple of feet, landing on the grass. But we were safe, and I lay there in silence, staring at the flames licking out of her balcony doors thirty feet above.

Did I just do what I think I did?

She was overwhelmed and tears of relief rolled down her cheeks. Wiping her eyes and nose with the back of her hand, she sat up.

"Thank you so much," she sobbed. "My god, that was so brave. Are you okay?"

I continued to lie on the grass, staring at the sky and contemplating what I'd done.

"I'm fine," I told her. "And you're welcome." I shook my head, laughing.

"What's so funny?"

"Well, I couldn't let you die, could I?"

She laughed too, but it was nervously. She knew how close she had come; how close we'd both come.

I stood up, dusted myself down and fumbled in my back pocket to make sure my passport was still intact.

"Come on," I said. "One more bit of climbing to do and then I'll take you to the paramedics for a once over.

I put my hands around her tiny waist and lifted her up so she could reach the top of the wall. I was right behind her and forced myself over, dropping down on the other side. She jumped down, steadying herself on me as she landed, and we walked slowly to the front of the hotel.

The scene was as I'd left it: police trying to hold back the hordes of people still waiting to find their loved ones and television crews and reporters filming the scene. The hotel was still ablaze but the fire-fighters had managed to get the majority of the ground floor under control. They were still on their knees, hoses wrapped around their arms and chests, dousing the remaining flames in the doorway.

I escorted the woman to an ambulance and a paramedic sat her down on the back step, wrapping a blanket around her shoulders. As he checked her over, I stepped away.

Even though what I'd just done could have cost me my life, my body and soul felt alive. Adrenaline rushed through me and my veins protruded like baby snakes between the tendons under my skin. I paced around, unable to settle, back and forth behind the ambulance. Glancing towards the front of the hotel, I saw some of the fire-fighters now on their feet, making their way into the building. My heart was thumping and the thrill and adventure of it all was all I could think about. I started to make my way across the grass but then heard her voice.

"Hey, they're taking me to the hospital."

Turning around, I saw the young woman's head peering out between the rear doors of the ambulance.

"You'll be fine," I said. "You're in good hands now."

"I just wanted to say thanks again. I'll never forget what you did."

"It's no problem," I told her.

The paramedic moved to close the doors, but the woman put her hand out, stopping him.

"What's your name?" she asked, smiling.

"Dave. What's yours?"

"Debbie," she said. "I really can't thank you enough. You saved my life."

I smiled at her as the doors closed. The paramedic thumped the back of the vehicle with his fist and with that, the sirens burst into life. Debbie was on her way to the hospital, safe and sound.

I should have gone with her, or at the very least, walked away, but the feeling of pride swelled in my chest. There I was on what looked like a movie set and I felt like James Bond — a hero of mine in my younger days. But this wasn't a movie, it was fucking real.

All thoughts of Rosa completely disappeared and the only thing in my mind was my one act of heroism. And I wanted more.

Without thinking of the repercussions, I began my journey towards the building.

The scenes that followed will live with me forever.

Chapter 11

PARALYSED

With the ambulance siren receding in the distance and Debbie safely on her way to the hospital, I nervously made my way to the hotel entrance. Every stride I took was with trepidation, my thoughts telling me to keep away. But I continued. Injured people lay on the grass with oxygen masks covering their shocked and frightened faces; woollen blankets had been wrapped around their shoulders, protecting them from the early morning chill. I walked past them and stepped cautiously into the building. Black smoke swirled above me and I covered my eyes with my left arm, holding my right out in front of me to find my way. And that's when it hit me... just then, that very second.

What the fucking hell am I doing?

But it was too late to turn back. The adrenaline had set in and I could feel it running through my veins. My blood pulsated and pumped through my body but I froze for a moment, looking around at the hotel guests. They were scared out of their skin, crying and coughing, their faces hollow and vacant and their eyes wide open in fear. I watched as they were led outside to safety with their arms slumped over the shoulders of the emergency crew. It spurred me on.

My pace quickened and I made my way through the foyer to the stairs. Still drunk, I stumbled over the first few steps of the curving marble stairway, steadied myself and clambered up to the first floor.

Two firemen ran past me as I turned right along the first floor corridor. Above me, small wooden beams began to peel away from the
ceiling and smoke leaked through the gaps they left behind. By reflex,
I ducked down several times to avoid being hit as I ran through the
corridor, stopping at each room for any sign of people, any sign of
life. I banged my fist on each door with my shirt partially covering
my face to protect me from the smoke.

"Is anybody in there?" I yelled. "Can anybody hear me?"

There was nothing. Silence. Not a fucking sound.

Further down the corridor and shadowed by the smoke, I saw someone; an elderly man wearing a dressing gown open to the waist, crawl-
ing on his hands and knees out of his room. He was facing the floor
and clutching his chest as he coughed uncontrollably.

"Please help me! I can't breathe."

I raced towards him.

"My eyes... I can't see... help me!" he said, gasping for air. His
dishevelled hair covered most of his face but when he lifted his head
I saw the terrified gaze in his weeping and bloodshot eyes. They bore
into me, as wide as saucers, from the thinness of his frightened face.
With my own watering eyes trying to focus, I knelt down beside him,
held his head in my arms and brushed his hair away from his face.

"I've got you," I told him. "Don't worry, I'll get you out."

He stuttered incoherently between sobs as his eyes filled with tears
and fell down his ashen face. I pulled the dressing gown cord tighter
around his waist and clasped my hand under his armpit.

"Is there anyone else in there?"

I tried to look inside the room, but couldn't see. His head was
flopping around as if he had no neck bones and as I lifted his limp
body from the floor, the urgency pervaded me.

"Sir, is there anyone else in the fucking room?"

"No. Just me... just me," he sobbed, grabbing hold of my shirt.

Taking hold of his arm and wrapping it around my shoulders whilst
I held on to his waist, he lifted his head. Frightened and scared, he
looked straight through me, his eyes filled with terror. Like a rabbit

caught in headlights, he knew he was mere moments away from death.

"I've got you," I said. "Now walk with me and I'll get you out of here, okay?"

"Yes. Thank you... thank you."

Struggling with his dead weight prevented me from moving as quickly as I wanted. He was a heavy man but I mustered enough strength from within — from somewhere — to carry him down the corridor. The sound of splintering wood emanated from above and I looked to make sure we weren't about to be hit by any falling beams. We turned left, back towards the staircase, and for a second I lost my footing and stumbled down the first few steps.

"I can't breathe," he gasped. "I can't breathe."

I tried to calm him down, holding onto the wall for support.

"We're nearly there okay? Come on, just a few more steps."

Several firemen loaded with breathing apparatus and other equipment passed us on the stairs going to the upper floors.

"Look. Look down there, see? Come on, it's not far now," I said, nodding towards the direction of the exit. "One more step, that's good... well done, only a few more feet."

The foyer floor was a collage of footprints — blackened boots and bare feet caught in a freeze-frame, telling the story of those who had fled across the once pearly- white tiles.

"Come on... last few feet and we're safe," I said, my voice becoming hoarser by the second from the intake of smoke.

Finally we reached the door.

Once outside I laid him gently on the grass, damp from the early morning dew. He immediately fell into convulsive bursts of weeping, coughing and spluttering as tears rolled down his cheeks. A female paramedic rushed over, wrapped a blanket around him and placed an oxygen mask over his face. I watched him, his eyes growing wider with each intake of breath he took, and I sat beside him, taking his hand in mine. For a big man he had small hands.

"Thank you," he mouthed through the mask, his voice barely a whisper.

"It's okay, it's okay," I told him, trying to catch my breath.

I blew out air from my dry, tasteless mouth and spread my arms out either side of me. Closing my eyes, I began to rock back and forth, my head a tangled mash of thoughts. Moments later, when I heard a deep, throaty laugh, I turned to look at him. Hot air had built up inside his mask and his kind, green eyes had softened.

"You saved my life," he croaked, pulling the mask away from his face. "How can I ever thank you?"

"You just did." I said, gently patting him on his back.

Wishing him well I stood up, ran my hand over my back pocket to check that my passport was still there, picked up a small bottle of water from the paramedic and walked away. As I twisted off the lid and clamped my mouth around the bottle, I turned around and smiled. He was being helped on to the back of the ambulance looking considerably better than he had ten minutes earlier. Taking small sips of water as if each one were my last, I watched as it sped off into the dawn.

That should have been it for me; time to move on, to go back to Rosa. I stared at the hotel — now reduced to little flickers of flames — and thought of what I'd done. I don't know if it was madness or stupidity, the lingering effects of the alcohol or the pride swelling in my chest. Perhaps it was a combination of them all. I'd saved two lives and that should have been enough, but it wasn't. I wanted more. Inhaling deeply and filling my lungs with the fresh morning air, I went back inside.

There was still a lingering hint of smoke sweeping around as I entered the foyer. Emergency crews were assisting people who were staggering and limping out of the hotel and I dashed past them and up the stairs, leaping over the last step to the first floor. I ran along the corridor stopping at each room to hammer on the door.

"Hello? Is anyone in there?"

There was no answer; no reply from any of them. I raced up another flight of stairs to the second floor and as I came to the top a policeman was there, on his way down, helping an injured woman to safety. His eyes fixed on mine with a prolonged stare that unnerved me and then, a second or two later, he carried on his way.

What the fuck was that about? I thought to myself.

I turned right onto the corridor and suddenly, as if I'd hit a brick wall, I stopped dead in my tracks. The blood drained from my face as a scene so horrific stretched out before me. I stumbled, open mouthed, and overcome with shock, fell back against the wall.

"Jesus Christ!" I said out loud.

Every muscle in my body stiffened — I literally couldn't move; I was paralysed with fear. There were three burnt, charred bodies; two female, both in the foetal position, their eyes wide open and their mouths screaming in silence, and one man, on his back, naked, his arms spread out by his side with his face to the right staring directly at me. There was no resemblance of the life that would have exuded from them only hours earlier. I had never seen a dead body before but never could I have imagined this. The expressions on their faces, scorched with fright from the terror they would have suffered, were horrific. An incredible sadness suddenly struck me and as tears filled my eyes I started to shake uncontrollably. I heaved, vomiting violently on the floor, unable to take in what I was seeing. I wiped my mouth with my shirt, took a huge deep breath as I tried to compose myself and then stepped over the bodies, looking straight ahead, determined to see if anyone else was alive.

I went from room to room, passing small pockets of flames that were still alive in the corridor, unable to get the bodies out of my mind. I came to room 267. The door was ajar and I kicked it open, walked inside and ran my hand along the walls, fumbling for a light-switch. I strained my ears for any sound, but heard nothing. Smoke still lingered above me as I took a few steps forward.

"Hello?" I called. "Is anyone in here?"

There was no answer. As my eyes adjusted to the dim light of the room I called again, this time with my hands around my mouth.

"Hello can anyone hear me?"

My voice bounced around the walls and returned nothing but a

mocking echo. I turned to leave but out of the corner of my eye I
noticed a large pile of loose change — a pyramid of coins a few feet
away on the bedside table. I walked over and without even thinking,
I gathered them up in two handfuls and stuffed them into my front
pockets. Beside the digital alarm clock was a passport. I picked it up
and flicked through it — an English name, the photo of a woman,
around fifty, attractive with dark hair. I hoped she had gotten out
okay. Tossing the passport back on the table, it disturbed two credit
cards which lay to the right of a small lamp. I can still remember the
smoke damaged, rose patterned shade that covered it. With my eyes
fixed on the cards, I noticed that the smoke was rapidly surrounding
me and I reacted without a thought. I picked up the cards and put
them in my back pocket. Immediately I felt ashamed, but my mind
was so mixed up with emotions and the desperation of the situation
that I didn't think of anyone or anything. I didn't think of the consequences. Shamefully, I hurried out of the room and closed the door
behind me without looking back.

Running down the corridor I considered going to the third floor
but I couldn't go on, it was impossible. My chest felt like it was on
fire and my lungs were about to explode. I had to get out. I continued
running until the three dead bodies appeared in front of me again.
I stopped, sickened. With my eyes looking straight ahead I held my
breath as I stepped over them again. The smoke was not as thick but
the corridor was dark, so stretching both my arms out in front of me
I navigated my way down the two flights of stairs. I stumbled and fell
down the last remaining marble steps with some coins and one of the
cards spilling out of my pocket and rolling across the floor. I left the
coins but picked up the card, shoving it into my front right pocket. I
pulled myself up and ran towards the exit, slipping and sliding on the
marble floor until finally, out of the hotel, I collapsed onto the grass.

I took heavy deep breaths, opening my mouth wide to get the
fresh air circulating around my lungs. My head was spinning but the
sensation of the air entering my body felt amazing. Closing my eyes,
I wiped the sweat from my face with my shirt sleeve, the images of

the charred bodies flooding back to haunt me. All I could picture was their faces staring back at me, their mouths hanging open and their eyes fixed in a deadened stare. The thought that they were someone's parent, someone's child, someone's brother or sister was too much to bear. Tears streamed from my eyes as the sadness overwhelmed me and I lay there a while, crying for the people I had never known and for the people who would never see them again.

The sun peeked out from the early morning clouds, warming my face and exposing the devastation around me. I lifted my aching body from the ground and stood up. There were still people — injured people — around the grounds of the hotel in need of help, so I walked back towards the front of the building. The coins in my pockets were heavy and uncomfortable so I scooped them out and placed them under a large grey stone in the rockery area of the hotel garden to collect later. I looked around at people crying and hugging their loved ones. Survivors with blankets around their shoulders were being ushered into the backs of ambulances and sadly, relatives were still searching, desperately hoping for their loved ones to come out alive. Reporters and their TV crews were preparing for the morning news bulletins.

An eerie stillness filled the air. The smouldering fire was now under control with just the odd disturbing crackle breaking the silence. At the front of the hotel, the injured were still being taken care of by the paramedics. A number of policemen leant against their cars, smoking and quietly talking with their colleagues whilst others monitored the surrounding scene. Tired firemen stood on guard, their once yellow uniforms saturated in black. With everything being taken care of, I sat cross-legged on the grass and watched, thinking about all that had happened in the past few hours. My mind raced, retracing every step I'd taken inside that building.

Suddenly, about ten feet to the left of me, a policeman started yelling at his colleagues and pointing at me. I recognised him... his eyes... those fucking eyes. He was the one who'd glared at me on the staircase. As he ran towards me, my heartbeat matched his every

step. Grabbing my arm, he hoisted me off the grass and marched
me towards his car.

"Hey, let go of me!" I said, trying to pull my arm from his grip.
"What's the problem?"

He ordered me to spread my arms on the roof of the car and forcefully kicked my legs apart. Reporters were looking in my direction
and he bellowed in my ear.

"You in hotel! I saw you running, running away!"

His English was bad, but I managed to understand it.

"Of course I was running! I was helping for fuck's sake. I was saving lives!"

"Shut the fuck up!" he spat, and then started laughing at me.

I was panicking. Did he see me steal the money and the cards? If so,
I was guilty of that. Hands up; I wanted to give it back there and then
but everything happened so quickly. He crouched down and searched
my legs up and down. Nothing. Then he searched my back pockets.
He pulled my passport out of my left pocket and the credit card
from my right. I turned around to look at him as he compared the
names on the card with my passport. My heart sank as I closed my
eyes, turned away and shook my head. Raising his hand, he forcefully
slapped the back of my head making my face hit the roof of the car
and then he kicked me. My knee buckled and he grabbed hold of
my arm, turning me around. I was facing him and those eyes kept
staring at me. His nose, flat and wide like a boxer's, was snarling
upwards as he ordered me to put my arms straight ahead with my
hands clasped. He handcuffed my wrists together and his colleague
took over, opening the back door of the police car and wrapping his
hand around my arms. With one push from behind, I fell head first
across the back seat. Somehow I managed to sit myself up and stared
into my lap at the cuffed hands resting between my legs.

Both policemen got into the front of the car and the driver flipped
the key in the ignition, bringing the engine to life along with the
radio. The policeman in the passenger seat turned his head, looked
at me and laughed.

"You English mother fucker," he said, then faced the front and continued to laugh with his colleague.

We sped off at full speed with the sound of the siren ringing in my ears, the cuffs cutting into my wrists and a single thought in my mind.

Dad was right.

The Spanish police were cunts.

Chapter 12

MIDNIGHT EXPRESS

Slumped in the back of the police car with my hands clamped together on my lap, I was emotionally and physically exhausted. As the car sped along the empty road, my head rocked rhythmically back and forth against the window, the blinding morning sun flashing in my eyes through the trees. My immediate thoughts were of my family. How the hell would I explain this to my parents? Where would I start? Sorry Mum and Dad, I've been arrested for stealing but I did save two lives. Is that okay? Do you forgive me?

Reality slapped me across the face as the policeman in the passenger seat turned his head and looked at me, his narrow eyes glaring at me like I was dirt. What an ugly fucker he was. He laughed — an evil, twisted, condescending chuckle.

"We go police station and sort you out, mother fucker!"

He turned away, still laughing, and continued his conversation with his side-kick. Their Spanish banter washed over me and I stared at the back of his head: his black hair unevenly cut just above his shirt collar and his thick, unshaven neck. As much as I tried to contain it, tears welled up in my eyes. I was petrified; I wanted to be at home with Mum, Dad, my brothers and Pink, not on my way to a police station. Again.

The handcuffs dug into me with every jolt and bump of the car

as we drove over potholes in the road. Shifting in the seat, I felt
something uncomfortable digging into my thigh and instantly I froze,
realising what it was. I still had a credit card in my front pocket.

Fuck.

I panicked, not knowing what the hell to do, but keeping an eye
on the men in front I managed to ease the card from my pocket. I
quickly shoved it between my knees with my mind racing. Should I
give it to them? Own up? And if I did, what would they do? If they
were going to slap me around a bit more I'd have to take it, but that
was the least of my worries. The last thing I wanted was to be in
even more trouble than I was already in.

Shit. Get out of this one, Dave, you idiot.

My eyes darted frantically around the car searching for somewhere
— anywhere — to put it. There were no floor mats to hide it under,
the window had no handles and there were no pockets in the side of
the doors. It was hopeless. I buried my head in my hands with my
nose inches from my knees, my tears flowing freely now and splashing
onto my jeans. That's when I saw it — an air vent just below the
seat and about three inches above the floor behind my legs. The
adrenaline kicked in immediately. I crouched forward a bit — hoping
to God they thought I was doing nothing more than crying — and
spreading my legs, I fumbled around the vent. There were three thin
slots and I managed to push the card into the middle one. Sitting
back, I breathed deeply with my heart thumping wildly in my chest.

The tyres squeaked as the car came to a halt at the station. The
driver got out, marched around the car to my side and opened the
door. He grabbed my arm, gestured for me to get out and with his
fingers squeezing into my flesh he dragged me across the forecourt
and into the building.

As we made our down the narrow hallway, I looked up. The arched
ceiling made me feel uncomfortable and claustrophobic and the small
leaded windows spaced out every three feet or so did little to brighten
the place. My every step was in synch with the square, red terracotta
tiles below the tread of my trainers. There were thirteen tiles and

thirteen steps — I counted each one of them — until suddenly there
was a holler behind us. The grip on my arm tightened and we stopped
at tile fourteen, turning around simultaneously.

"You fucking Englishman, you motherfucker. You're a son of a
prostitute, you motherfucker!"

My heart sank as I saw the other policeman standing in the doorway, his arm held up with the card in-between his thumb and finger.
So much for my hiding place. He slammed shut the door and ran
towards us, shouting and swearing. His face was over tanned and
he had deep engraved lines on his forehead. He wasn't tall, just an
inch or so shorter than me, but he was stocky with big arms and
big hands. Taking a hold of my other arm, they both escorted me
to the end of the hallway with my handcuffed wrists rigid in front
of me. I was still counting and there were thirty six steps and thirty
six tiles before we reached a shabby, gun-metal door. The policeman
to my right fumbled with the bunch of keys attached to his trouser
belt and swearing and cursing he attempted but failed miserably to
open it. Eventually, on the third attempt he succeeded, and they led
me down another dank corridor, their pace quickening with each and
every step. The natural light was fading fast behind me as we turned
right, went down three flights of stairs and came to a basement.
Another door was opened and the stench from the room hit me with
a vengeance; the smell of stale sweat, urine and shit in that order.
There was no natural light; just two fluorescent tubes hanging above
me by a cable. Flies buzzed all around, bouncing off the lights in a
state of frenzy. Many were dead inside, their black bodies sucking
away the light.

Men with angry, dirty faces and wide, bloodshot eyes stretched
their arms through the bars of their cells, trying to touch me and
grab me as we passed them. They were like wild animals, shouting
and screaming in a language I didn't understand. The policemen
thrashed their truncheons against the bars, swiping out and hitting
arms that were in their way. I was terrified; I felt sick. The noise
vibrating off the cold grey concrete walls as they continued to shout

was horrendous.

We came to a double cell at the back of the room. They told me to stand still and I did; I froze. One policeman unlocked the cell and opened the door while the other crouched down to untie and remove my shoelaces. My handcuffs were released and they shoved me into the cell where I landed face down on a cold, wet concrete floor. The cell door slammed shut and the key turned and locked as I lay motionless on the floor. As their footsteps faded, I continued to lay face down with my eyes closed, trying desperately to contain my emotion. I could feel the damp of the floor seeping through my shirt and the pungent smell of days gone by — month's old urine — flooded my nostrils. I buried my nose deep into my arm as the screaming and shouting continued around me. I didn't fucking want to be there. Please let me open my eyes and be somewhere else. Please! But the noise just wouldn't go away. I was there and it was real. I was living a fucking nightmare.

Pulling myself together, I lifted my head, looked straight ahead and unfolding my arms with my palms on the floor, I forced myself up and struggled to my feet. There was a shadow of a man before me, to my right, and before I had time to get myself up I felt his boot in my ribcage. I buckled over, shouting out in pain, and as his shadow slowly disappeared back to the opposite end of the cell, I collapsed back onto the floor. Taking in some deep breaths, I crawled towards the corner of the cell, sat up, curled my knees up to my face and buried my head between them. With my hands over my ears to shut out the cries from the other prisoners, I rocked back and forth, unable to comprehend what was happening.

Unaware of how much time had passed, the sound of clanging keys made me look up. A guard was doing his rounds pulling a metal trolley behind him and he crouched down placing two oranges and two plastic cups of water on the floor, a foot away from the bars. Out of the corner of my eye I noticed movement in the opposite corner and I watched as my cell mate stood up and limped towards the door. I couldn't help but hope that he'd got hurt from kicking me, the bastard. He was dirty with ripped jeans and a torn black tee shirt, over six foot tall, with a tough leathery face and yellow rotten teeth. His small bloodshot eyes looked around, like he was searching for danger, but he was only looking for his share. He picked up his orange and water and limped back to his corner of the cell without looking at me. When he was still, I stood up and slowly walked towards the door for mine, my loose trainers slopping around on my feet. I grabbed my cup and orange and retreated to my corner with the horrible taste of smoke still in my mouth. I peeled the orange with my dirty hands, the dirt from my nails smudging across its skin. I thought of the son of Elvis as I removed the pith, separated the segments and ate each one as slowly as I could, enjoying the delicious, sweet taste on my tongue. Once I'd finished, I picked up the plastic cup and drank the luke-warm warm water in one mouthful, but it did little to quench my thirst. I stuffed the orange peel into the empty cup beside me. Exhausted and weak, I just wanted to sleep and to forget about this nightmare, and I curled up on the cold damp concrete floor, facing the wall with my hands wrapped around me and my knees to my chest, counting out loud to try and silence the cries around me. I thought of Rosa and eventually I slept.

Suddenly there was the clanging of metal — a baton hitting the metal bars as the guard went from one cell to the next. Prisoners shouted to each other across the room, their voices echoing off the walls. It took a moment or two to get my bearings. What time was it? What day was it? Where the fuck was I? The guard opened each cell and put more oranges and water on the floor. He spoke Spanish to the prisoners, laughing and shouting, taunting them. They replied with finger signs, spitting at him as he walked past. I waited for my cell mate to collect his and then I collected mine. Again I peeled the orange, split it in two and ate a half at a time. Then I drank the water, luke-warm as before. I put the peel in the empty plastic cup and placed it against the wall. There were two cups filled with orange peel, side by side.

To make the time pass I'd throw each slice of peel and see how many I could get into the cup. My best score was seven on the trot; my lucky number. I'd sit with my back against the wall, legs stretched out in front of me, eyes closed and my hands covering my ears. I'd never done it before but I prayed to God for the first time in my life. Please God get me out of here. Please God... This routine must have carried on for a few days because I had eight empty plastic cups complete with orange peel against the wall. My highest score got to 13. Not my lucky number at all.

After many prayers and quite literally on the brink of madness, the basement door opened and a guard walked towards my cell. He stopped, opened the cell door and motioned me to stand up. I managed with difficulty, kicking over the plastic cups and scattering the orange peel across the floor. I approached him, holding onto the wall for support, when he suddenly reached out and grabbed me, forcing my arms behind my back. He handcuffed me and marched me out of the cell, past the screaming prisoners and into another room along the corridor. He pushed open the door of a small room, let it slam behind him and sat me down at a desk. The room was bare: no pictures, just a window with metal bars on the bottom and a sliver of glass along the top that let in the only natural light — a narrow slant of sunshine and a tiny glimpse of the world outside. The room was lit by a single bulb hanging from the ceiling. The door opened and I heard the clack of a woman's footsteps behind me. The smell of her scent wafted past me as she walked past and sat down opposite me behind the desk.

"Remove the handcuffs," she told the guard. He obliged and returned to stand by the door.

Massaging my wrists, I looked up at her. She was attractive and wearing a dark blue, two piece suit with a white blouse. Her hair was dark and in a ponytail. She was Spanish but spoke perfect English.

"Hello. My name is Carmela and I am a lawyer for the Spanish Consulate."

She showed me her business card and I nodded.

"How are you?"

"Could be better." I leant forward on the chair. "Why am I here? I haven't done anything wrong. Really. I swear."

She didn't answer me.

"I hope you've been treated well."

I raised my eyebrows at her.

A smirk appeared across her face. "You remind me of someone."

"Really? Who?"

"Brad Davies."

"The actor? How strange, cos I feel a bit like him at the moment."

A wry smile appeared on her thin red-lined lips. "Okay, let's continue with your case. I'm here to inform you of the next procedure." She opened a brown file which was on the desk in front of her.

They already have a file on me?

"Tomorrow morning at 9:00am, you will be appearing in court to face the Judge who will inform you of the charges against you." She looked up at me as she clasped her hands together and laid them on the file.

"What are the charges?" My hands began to sweat and I wiped my forehead as I shifted in the chair.

She turned to the guard, gave a quick nod of her head, and then looked straight into my eyes. "You are being charged with theft, arson and manslaughter."

I sat bolt upright. "What do you mean arson and manslaughter? I saved fucking lives! I risked my own fucking life!" I stood up to protest. "I didn't start the fire; I was at a party. I didn't do anything...I didn't." I went to move towards the desk but the guard was behind me with his hands on my shoulders in an instant, forcing me to sit back down. He took hold of my arms and handcuffed me. Carmela closed the file and motioned the guard to take me away.

Chapter 13

CUPS AND ORANGES

The sound of jangling keys stirred me from my sleep and I opened my eyes to see the eight plastic cups lined against the concrete wall. I stared at the orange peel, now shriveled and dehydrated, and couldn't help but wonder if I looked the same. I certainly felt it. Don't they ever clean this shithole? I thought, pulling myself from the floor.

A burly guard with a nasty, toothless grin unlocked my cell door and took the familiar metal tray from his trolley, his short sleeved shirt exposing his thick, tattooed arms. A dragon traced its way from wrist to elbow on his left arm whilst a snake did the same on his right. I watched the brown and black scales of the snake move and twitch as he placed our food and drink on the floor before locking the door. We were his last call, and as he strode past the other prisoners he gave them all the same toothless stare.

The walls echoed as he slammed the heavy door behind him and turned the key. It had been four or five days but I still couldn't get used to that sound. I stood up and gingerly walked over to get my share, somewhat surprised that there was only one orange and one plastic cup. My first thought was that I'd have a fight on my hands and I looked around for my cellmate, preparing myself. But he was gone. Whether he'd been freed, moved or taken to court didn't interest me in the slightest — I really didn't give a shit and was glad to have the place to myself. I wondered when they'd taken him though, and tried to recall the previous few hours. Most of it was a blur; endless hours of nothingness interspersed with shouting and sleep.

I felt disorientated and weak as I made my way back to the corner of what was now my cell. My stomach was in a constant state of unrest, a combination of hunger and nervous anticipation about what the day would hold. Over and over, my head pounded with Carmela's words: "manslaughter and arson." Feeling sick I sat down, crossed my legs and peeled off the orange skin. Very slowly, one by one, I separated the segments. The longer I took eating the orange the further I was away from meeting the Judge at the Court House. "Manslaughter and arson." The words circled around my head.

The orange was sour and I spat most of it out along with the pips, firing them into the cups. The water was a welcoming taste though — even warm, it drowned out the bitterness in my mouth. I finished it in three gulps and placed the cup alongside the others. Nine plastic cups. Apart from Carmella, I hadn't spoken to anyone in days, so the only communication I'd had was with myself. At times I even spoke to the cups, and as stupid as it sounds now, I had a name for each one. Each day there were another two cups; each day two new members of a growing family.

My eyes were heavy and tired from another sleepless night of tossing and turning on the damp, concrete floor. I wiped some sticky sleep away from my eyes and rubbed it onto my jeans. I hadn't changed them since I'd left the hostel which seemed like a lifetime ago and even though Rosa had washed them for me, they now smelt of smoke, piss and shit, as did my shirt. I was in desperate need of a shower.

I looked around at the other prisoners who were unusually quiet. Some stood with their arms hanging out between the cell bars, smoking and staring at each other, whilst others had their heads down, staring at the floor. I had no doubt that they were all wondering when they would ever be getting out of there, as was I. Looking around I tried to take it all in: vulnerable men — incarcerated for whatever reason — not having a clue about what the next day would bring. Just looking at them, I felt sorry for them. I thought of my family: my mum, dad, brothers and sister. What the hell would they think if they knew? Did they know? Had anyone told them? I felt my stomach fall and did all that I could to contain it.

Sometime later, the clanking of keys and the turning of the lock made me look up and I stared across the cell as the basement door opened. The same, toothless guard appeared. Passing the other cells, he marched towards me, occasionally lashing out at the arms of the prisoners with his baton, still smiling that fucking ugly grin of his as he did so. What a bastard. The prisoners he hit yelled out in pain, but they still spat back at him, most times managing to connect with the side of his face and the back of his neck. It looked like a sick and twisted game; one I didn't understand at first. But it was obvious they were asserting the last bit of freedom they had left — the one thing the guards couldn't take away.

When he reached my cell door he fumbled for the key on his belt. I was surprised he could find any keys at all; he was grossly overweight with an enormous stomach that hung down over his blue uniformed trousers. When he located the right one and opened the door, he pointed at me with two fingers and he told me to get up. "Jesus... here goes," I muttered to myself. As I stood, he approached me, grinning as he did so and wiping salvia from his face. He tossed two white laces onto the floor and I knelt down and picked them up. Taking both ends of each lace, I carefully measured them and pushed them through each eyelet of my trainers one at a time — first my left and then my right. He shouted at me to hurry up and with fright I glanced up at him. With the baton in one hand, he was hitting the palm of his other, his grin diminished to an evil stare. I hurriedly finished tying them and stood up. We were nose to nose. "Fuck," I said, turning away. His breath was rancid.

It occurred to me that the last time I'd cleaned my teeth was at Rosa's apartment, days earlier. Cupping my hand over my mouth, I blew into it and inhaled. It was just as bad, but at least I had an excuse. Thoughts of Rosa whirred around in my mind. Why didn't I just go back to you? Why the fuck did I go back into the hotel?

Suddenly, the guard took hold of both my arms, turned me around and shoved me into the wall. With all thoughts of Rosa lost, the side of my face rebounded off the concrete and I felt warm blood trickle from my lip as the plastic cups splayed across the floor. Grabbing hold of my wrists, he pulled them together around my back and handcuffed me. "Why the fuck do you have to be so rough, you bastard!" I yelled, but he just laughed, his heavy breath sliding down the back of my neck.

He marched me out of the cell, slamming the door behind us. We strode past the other prisoners who whistled and clapped, trying to reach out and grab me by my shirt. He opened the door and we made our way along the corridor, past the room where I'd met Carmela, up three flights of stairs and along the narrow hallway with the arched ceiling. I felt uncomfortable and claustrophobic again — even more so knowing where we were heading. The windows, now to my right, were letting in the early morning light. The sun was out and I hadn't seen natural light for days. He gripped my arm as we walked to the end of the corridor, his tattooed snake staring at me as I looked down and counted the tiles out loud again — thirty six, exactly the same number of steps and tiles as before.

The guard fumbled for the key and I wondered again how he ever managed to see over his stomach, but in one attempt he found it and unlocked the door. When the bright morning sun hit my eyes, I instantly turned away and looked down, unable to cover my eyes because of the handcuffs. The sensation of the heat was incredible and for a moment I was transported — a beautiful vision of Rosa and I on the beach playing out in my mind. But it was short-lived.

A blue police van screeched to a halt in front of us and the driver jumped out and unlocked the two back doors. The guard yanked me onto the pavement and then onto the road.

There was a caged door between the door and the back of the van. He opened it and I felt the full force of his hands on my back as he pushed me inside. I managed to steady myself and slumped down onto an empty seat to my left. There were four other male prisoners in the back of the van, all staring at me, and when they started to shout at me I was relieved that they were handcuffed too.

I couldn't understand why there was so much hatred towards me. Was it because I was English? Had they heard about my charges? Shifting my body, I turned my back to ignore them as the driver turned the key in the ignition, and as the engine came to life and we made our way to the court, I stared out of the window watching the world rush by, terrified of what lay ahead.

Chapter 14

THE JOURNALIST

The morning sun warmed my face as I peered through the small, van window at the cloudless blue sky above. Varying shades of green covered the countryside, the hedges and fences turning the fields into a life-size jigsaw. Buildings were scattered across the land and as we passed the occasional farmer, I caught glimpses of them tending to their livestock and harvest. My mind wandered from farmhouse to farmhouse, imagining the design of the interior of the properties. Do they have a large reception room? Is there a wood burner? Is it a typical farm style kitchen? My property background kicked in and I was in my element. I wanted to be back in my office negotiating deals and viewing properties in Central London, but that seemed like a lifetime away. Reality hit me when one of the prisoners kicked the back of my right leg. I turned around and he laughed at me — they all did — and he muttered something in Spanish. Whatever it was, I ignored it, and turned my back on them. He never kicked me again.

We passed an old working windmill with cows alongside it, some standing and others laying down and chewing their cud. When the sun disappeared behind a cloud, I caught a reflection of myself in the window, my hair dishevelled and matted, not glossy and shiny how Pink always liked it. I stared back at myself — at my eyes lost and scared, and at the black circles sucking the life from them. My face was thin and tired, my tan had faded fast and I didn't recognize myself anymore. Who was I? What had I become? I looked a complete mess. Closing my eyes, my head drooped like a drunk in his final minutes of consciousness and a tear slid down my cheek onto my week old beard. I tried my best to look past the glass and up to the sky but when we entered a tunnel, the daylight vanished. For those few seconds, with the light and warmth gone, I felt more alone than I had ever done in my life. Another tear fell from my cheek onto the dirty window and I followed its path as it zigzagged downwards and finally disappeared into the condensation on the glass. For a moment or two I was totally lost.

The van took a sharp right and my head bounced off the window, rousing me from my day dream. The fields had gone and I stared out at rows of cafés, at people drinking coffee and waiters rushing back and forth with their orders. When the van turned again and slowed down, I immediately saw the imposing court house in front of me. A small congregation of well-dressed people were standing, talking and smoking outside, their briefcases at their feet. The Georgian style building covered four floors and the white pillars either side of the large, oak wood doors were guarded by two policemen talking casually, absorbed in their own gossip. Large stash windows were evenly placed in equal sets of two across all the floors — each set displaying a range of pretty spring flowers beneath them. It looked too beautiful to be a court house.

We drove past the crowd, turned right and stopped by the side of the building. I heard some footsteps going around the side and then to the back of the van and bright sunshine flooded in as the rear doors opened. A guard ordered us to get off. The other prisoners left one by one and still handcuffed, I manoeuvred myself upright, jumped onto the step and onto the road. The heat hit me instantly and reminded me of the moment I'd first arrived in Spain and stepped off of the plane.

We were ushered through the side door into the hallway of the Court House — a large space which seemed a lot smaller with the bustle of people and activity. With a guard by my side, we walked along the hallway and I was escorted up the court's elegant marble stairway to the first floor. As we made our way along the corridor I noticed a small group of people to my right, whispering to each other and staring and pointing at me. The atmosphere became tenser as their whispers grew louder.

"There's the guy who started the fire!" One young girl shouted.

"There's the bastard, he's the one who did it!" said another, yelling and pointing at me as we passed them.

I tried to plead my innocence. "I didn't start the fire! I didn't do anything. It's a mistake! They have it all wrong." But my voice was lost amid theirs; it was pointless.

The guard tightened his grip on my arm and we hurriedly marched down the hallway leaving the crowd behind. We came to a closed room with a chair outside and the guard pointed for me to sit down and told me not to move. I did as he asked, lowered my head and stared at the floor, trying my best to ignore the accusations that were being bellowed from the end of the hallway. Glancing up, I noticed a clock on the wall with its large black numbers confirming the time. It was eight thirty.

A man with blond receding hair and round silver rimmed glasses, smartly dressed in beige trousers and a plain blue shirt, sat down next to me.

"So, you're the guy who started the fire?"

Looking straight into his eyes, and through gritted teeth, I replied: "look, I don't know who the fuck you are, but…"

"I'm Paul," he interrupted, offering me his hand.

"No chance," I replied. I leant forward, showing him my arms cuffed behind my back.

"Ah yes. I see. Of course not." He pulled his hand away.

"I didn't start the fire," I told him. "I wasn't even there. I was at a party with my girlfriend. I needed some air, left the party on my own, went for a walk and saw the flames in the distance. Stupidly, I went to have a look. I didn't start it, I swear. I'm being accused of arson and manslaughter, it's fucking crazy. This is wrong. It's all wrong."

"Okay, okay," he said, patting my shoulder and standing up." Look, just give me a minute."

He walked over to a guard who was standing, legs astride, outside the closed door. They spoke in Spanish for a few moments and I watched as the guard nodded. Paul returned and sat down.

"Okay, Dave, he's agreed I can talk with you. And I'm going to try and get the judge to agree to me representing you in court."

"How can you help me? Are you a lawyer?"

"Not exactly," he said. "I'm a journalist for an English national newspaper. I've been living here for quite a few years and I'm well known within the court system. I've helped lots of people who have got into trouble overseas."

"Well if that's the case," I said, "can you start by getting me out of these bloody handcuffs?"

He nodded, then stood up and walked back over to the guard. Within seconds, the guard came over, grabbed hold of my arm, lifted me from the chair and removed the cuffs. I gently rubbed my wrists as we both sat down again.

"Dave, you look like crap," Paul said. "And you smell even worse."

I didn't flinch; he was right.

"I understand you've been held in a cell for about week without washing facilities and proper food."

"Yep, not the five star treatment I had in mind." I managed a laugh for the first time in days.

"This is the plan, Dave," he said. "I'm going to ask the judge for bail and request that whilst on bail you stay with me."

"Fuck, really?" I looked at him, my eyes wide. "Shit. I'm sorry to swear, but would I really get bail because I can't face going back to the cells again...I just can't take that place anymore."

"I can't promise, but I'll do my best."

"Why are you doing this for me?"

"Because..." he said, placing his hands on his lap, "...I believe you and this is what I do."

"Thanks," I said, "I need all the help I can get. And now the cuffs are of. . . " I offered him my hand and he shook it.

The guard moved away from the door as it opened. My name was called and we both stood up and made our way to the court room. Just before we entered, Paul stopped me and took me to one side.

"Dave, listen to me. This is a preliminary hearing, like a trial before the trial. The judge is going to decide whether you're guilty or not and whether there's enough evidence to force you to stand trial. If so, he'll set a date. The Judge will ask you to acknowledge and confirm your name. Just answer him yes, with a smile. Also, if he asks you if you understand the charges, just say yes, nothing else. Then I'll speak on your behalf and let's hope he agrees to what I ask."

"Okay," I said, but Paul. . . "

He turned and looked at me.

"Just get me bail."

"I'll do my best. Come on, let's go."

Even before I'd put a foot in the room, the guard grabbed my arm and handcuffed my wrists again and marched me through with Paul following behind us. The room was large and airy with one huge window that had a venetian blind pulled half way down to block out some of the morning sun. A ceiling fan rotated and purred, circulating warm air around the room. Three men, all in their fifties I guessed, and looking impressive in matching tailored pinstripe suits, had their heads down, writing and shuffling papers behind their desks, facing the elevated seat at the front of the court room. A smart woman with a pretty face was to my left, tapping the keyboard of her typewriter as I was escorted to the dock. Paul headed towards the right hand-side of the room and sat on the first bench, just behind the three men.

The long hand of the clock on the wall opposite me moved towards the twelve and the short hand to the nine. Right on time, the Judge — in a dark black suit with a matching cloak over his shoulders — appeared from a back office. Everyone in the room stood. He was a tall, slim man with a neat grey hair style and a lined, pale face. He sat down behind his desk and we followed suit. Then one of the

men stood up, called for the case to commence and motioned for
me to stand. I obliged, feeling ashamed and nervous, with my heart
thumping in my chest.

"Please can you confirm your name," the Spanish Judge requested
in excellent spoken English.

"David Paul Perlmutter," I answered with a slight stutter. I hadn't
stuttered since I was a kid.

"I've looked at your file and all the correspondence with it and the
final decision is that a hearing will take place regarding the charges
against you. Do you understand the charges against you?"

I felt the rush of blood in my head. The room closed in on me as
I looked at Paul for help.

"Do you understand the charges against you and why you are
here?" he repeated.

I thought about what Paul had told me to say, but the charges —
arson and manslaughter — I did not understand. I looked at Paul
again and noticing that I was panicking, he stood up.

"May I speak with the accused, Your Honour?" Paul asked the
Judge.

"Yes," he said, confirming it with a nod of his head.

"Paul," I whispered. I can't answer that question. I don't understand the charges. I know I'm guilty of theft, but arson and
manslaughter? No way. I'm innocent."

"Listen to me, Dave." His voice was stern. "Just answer yes to the
questions because if you don't, you may not get bail. It's up to you,
but I'll help you, I promise."

I turned back to the Judge. "Yes your Honour, I told him. "I understand the charges."

"You may sit down then."

He turned away from me and scanned the file on his desk. Turning
a page, he asked one of the men in front of him to come forward.
They were in deep conversation for a few minutes and then they
called Paul over. Paul looked in my direction and smiled. Another
few minutes later the Judge announced that Paul would say a few

words on my behalf.

"Your honour, I would like to request that until the trial commences, the accused resides with me where I will look after him and prepare him to be ready for the court case. He has been in jail at the police station for a week or so without having a wash or a decent meal. I will guarantee that he comes to court when the case begins. I hope this is acceptable, Your Honour."

I looked around the room while the Judge deliberated the request, my heart beating fast. I had an itchy spot on my nose but couldn't scratch it as my sweaty palms were still handcuffed behind my back. The pretty woman tapped busily away on her typewriter and after a few moments, the Judge looked up from his desk, took off his glasses and turned towards me.

"The court grants you bail under the conditions that you remain under Paul's guidance and that he brings you back to court when the case commences in... now let's see..." He placed his glasses on the tip of his nose, looked down at his desk and said, "...three days from today at nine am. Do you understand?"

With total relief I answered: "Yes Your Honour, I do. Thank you."

"You may step down. We will see you in seventy two hours." He closed the file.

Everyone stood in unison as the Judge left his seat and returned to his office.

As I stood down from the dock, the guard released the cuffs. I felt free for the very first time.

I told you I'd help you," Paul said, shaking my hand. "I just have to sign a form for your release, get your passport and then we can go. Give me two minutes."

I didn't say anything. I couldn't. I was in a trance. I'd just been granted bail for arson and manslaughter! I had seventy two hours until the beginning of the case. I kept repeating in my head: bail for arson and manslaughter. I was exhausted and sat down on the nearest bench in an emotional daze.

To my right, the three men in their pin stripe suits were sitting behind their desks, organizing their files and paperwork for the next hearing. To their left, the attractive woman was still typing, her long legs stretched out with the tips of her shoes just visible beneath her desk. Paul was sitting down and signing something, then he stood up, shook hands with one of the men and walked towards me, slipping my passport into his shirt breast pocket.

"Okay Dave, let's get out of here," he said. "Let's get you cleaned up and fed."

I smiled and thanked him, the relief washing over me. We left the room, walked past the guard, along the corridor, down the stairs and out of the building.

The hostile crowd had thankfully vanished and we turned right, heading towards the car park. Moments later I was in the front seat of Paul's car and on my way to his apartment.

Chapter 15

THE PROMISE

Paul's apartment was on the third floor of a small complex surrounded by palm trees and lush green gardens. The large terrace overlooked the town centre with a distant view of the sea. It was modern, built only two years before with pure white walls throughout and cream wood work. There were two double bedrooms, two bathrooms, a nice size reception room and a fully fitted kitchen. As we'd driven back from the court I'd noticed new developments being built everywhere; it was a booming time in property, Paul had mentioned in the car. It was a subtle reminder of my previous life and I walked around the place with a hint of jealousy; it was only a few months earlier that I'd had a similar apartment back in London. But there I was — crashing on a stranger's sofa in Spain, on bail for arson and manslaughter and with a court case to look forward to in three days' time.

My mind was racing faster than Ayrton Senna down the home straight as I felt the full force of the hot water pouring over my body in the shower. My eyes closed as the water cascaded off my face with the events of the past few days hitting me. I was scared; really scared. A few tears escaped and became lost in the falling water as I stood with my head down and the hot steam surrounding me. I turned the water off, opened the frosted glass sliding door, stepped out and began to dry myself. I wiped the steam away from the mirror with my left palm and a pair of dark brown eyes stared back at me. I became lost within the black pupils for a while and felt dizzy and light headed. Taking a step back, I stared at the smearing of facial features all over the mirror's surface. Drops of water fell from my wet hair onto my shoulders and as I hand dried my hair, I noticed my hairline in the mirror. Had it receded even more or was it just the smears I was seeing? I ignored it and in desperate need of a shave, I looked around for some razors but couldn't find any. Thinking that Paul could help me out, buttoning my shirt and with my jeans rolled up just past my ankles, I went to the kitchen to find him. He wasn't there, but there was a note with a key on the worktop.

Hi Dave, I hope you're feeling better after the shower. I had to go out. Help yourself to food. The key is for the front door if you want to stretch your legs. I'm back this later this afternoon. We'll chat later. Paul.

The writing was a mixture of scribbles, lines, letters and dots, but I managed to understand. That's nice of him, I thought, putting the key into my pocket.

The water came rushing out of the chrome mixer taps as I filled the kettle and switched it on. Now, what can I have to eat? I said it out loud as I opened the fridge, relieved that there wasn't a single orange in sight. I took a box of eggs, a packet of ham, some cheese and tomatoes and placed them on the worktop. The steam from the kettle screamed out of the funnel as the water reached boiling point and automatically deactivated with a noise that made me jump. Get a grip, Dave, I told myself. I poured the boiling water into a mug that had a Barcelona football badge printed on it and added some coffee, milk and sugar. As I stirred it, my thoughts turned to Paul. Why is he being so helpful? He's not a lawyer; he's a journalist for a national paper. Does he want a story? Is this why he's helping me?

I cracked three eggs into a bowl, stirred them with a fork then poured the mixture into a sizzling frying pan along with the tomatoes, ham and cheese. I grabbed the mug of coffee and perched on the edge of a stool, the questions racing around my mind. I slid the omelette onto a plate and began to eat, closing my eyes as I devoured each and every mouthful.

I drank the coffee and made another.

As I finished washing the dishes, the thoughts in my mind began to manifest and all I could think about was that in seventy hours I'd be facing charges of manslaughter and arson. I needed some air, some time to think, but time was my enemy — I could almost hear the ticking of the clock counting down the minutes to my trial. Finding my trainers, I slipped them on and headed down the hallway, passing various rooms on my way. One of them had its door ajar and I glanced in, noticing a passport on the bedside table. I knocked on the door, a habit of mine, paused for a few moments then stepped inside. When I opened the passport and saw my own face staring back at me, I was stunned at how much I'd changed in the three years since it was taken. I looked at myself with a sense of longing for the person I used to be, placed it back on the table and left the room.

Having had more than enough of confined spaces, I took the stairs instead of the lift down to the ground floor. Concrete walls followed me as I walked down the three floors — thirty eight steps, another new habit of mine — to the bottom. I pushed open the glass double-doors, stepped out onto the pavement and had to shield my eyes from the strong rays of the afternoon sun. The warmth hitting my face and body was a feeling that I'd forgotten and I stood for a moment, my eyes closed in a trance, with my arms by my side. I was lost in the moment until a car sped past, the wind catching my face, and then the moment vanished.

The pavements were bursting with tourists and the cafés and restaurants were full to the brim with lunchtime diners. They were all undoubtedly enjoying their holiday without a care in the world, but with each step I took I felt they were looking at me — talking about me with their whispering voices. Very quickly I became un-comfortable and paranoid and quickened my pace as I back tracked, hesitating as I passed Bar Lolita. It was the place where my first gig was with Kelvin and Anthony and again I was reminded of how different things could have been had I made different choices. It was unsettling — the knowledge that a split second decision can completely change the course of someone's life.

I hurried along the side of the road until I came to Paul's apartment block, ran up the three flights of stairs — not counting this time — and turned the key of the door, closing it behind me. My heart was thumping and with sweat running down the side of my face, I closed my eyes and leant back against the door.

I had to do something.

The Spanish weather bulletin on TV had just finished and the presenter was placing sun images on the Spanish map, confirming that it would be another hot afternoon. I stretched out on the sofa, clenched all the muscles in my body, counted to ten, and let out a huge sigh. My eyelids were getting heavier and within a matter of seconds, they were closed. I lay there until the drone of the TV became a comforting hum and within moments I was asleep.

"Dave, Dave, wake up."

I let out a moan as I slowly opened my eyes and saw Paul in front of me.

"I'm back. Did you sleep well?"

"Hi, um. . . yes, thanks," I replied, turning away and slowly closing my eyes again.

"Hey, come on, wake up. I'll make some coffee and then we can talk, okay?"

"Okay, white, one sugar," I said wondering why he was in such a hurry.

I was half asleep when he returned from the kitchen and placed a mug on the table next to me.

"So, do you want to talk about what happened?" he asked, staring at me.

I sat up, yawned out loud and reached over to get the mug, taking a sip of my coffee.

"So you're a journalist."

"Yes, I am, like I told you. But I want you to tell your side of the story."

I took another sip, my eyes caught by a painting of the Marbella Marina, just above the fireplace opposite me, reminding me of Rosa and the night of the party.

"Look at me," Paul snapped.

My eyes fixed on his. "Why should I talk to you? Papers never print the fucking truth, do they?"

"For fuck's sake Dave. I've helped you, haven't I? You're on bail. Why would I write something that isn't true? I promise mate, just tell me your side and only that will be printed. Nothing else, okay?"

The sunlight flowed through the large balcony windows as the temperature increased. I wondered if it was just me feeling the heat or if the weather girl had actually been right for once, but when Paul stood up and walked over to the kitchen to turn the air conditioning on, it answered my question.

"Dave, come on, it'll be good for you to let it all out."

"Okay, okay, but you'll only print what I tell you? Nothing else?

"Agreed."

Paul sat back on the black leather chair, got out his pad and pen and started to take notes.

I told him about the party with Rosa and when Peter had turned up drunk. I also told him in detail about how I saved Debbie and the rescue of the old man.

"I wonder how they're doing?" I said. "Better than me, I hope."

"Christ, I didn't know about that."

"You didn't? But you're a journalist."

"Yes, I am. And this is what I do — I find the truth. So tell me your story and I'll help."

"Well, I certainly need some," I said, finishing my coffee.

Placing the empty mug on the table next to me, I began to tell Paul what happened next.

"After the ambulance drove the old man away, I went back inside. I felt invincible at the time — crazy I know — but that's how it was."

I paused. "Do you have anything stronger to drink?"

"JD?"

I nodded.

He placed a full bottle of Jack Daniels on the table and poured two glasses. I drank mine in one gulp.

"Thanks, I needed that."

He poured me another.

"Cheers." I said raising the glass, taking a sip and continuing.

"I passed two or three firemen helping people out and then I went to the first floor, but there was no one there, so I went up to the second. There was a copper there just staring at me. He freaked me out."

I took another sip of the drink.

"Go on, what happened next?" Paul said, flipping over the page of his pad.

"I turned the corner and fuck..."

I grabbed the bottle and filled my glass.

"Right in front of me, three bodies. Lifeless. Dead." I paused, swallowing the emotion rising in my throat. "I'd never seen a dead body before."

With his head down, Paul didn't look up at me as he continued to write.

"I felt sick. I just stood there and stared at them. It'll haunt me forever."

"Did you look for anybody else?"

"Yes. I stepped over the bodies... I had no choice... and went from room to room looking for people. Then I came to a room with the door open so I went inside and shouted to see if anyone was there. I was about to leave when I saw some change on the table."

I took another few sips.

"I'm not proud of what I'm gonna say now, Paul." I felt the prickle of tears in the corners of my eyes.

"It's okay," Paul said calmly. "Just take a deep breath and let it all out."

Another sip of whisky passed my lips.

"I took the cash — all coins — and two credit cards. I wasn't thinking. I was desperate and...oh, I don't know...I was in a state. I'd been through a lot that night Paul. You know that now."

"We've all done stupid things that we've regretted."

"I know. But taking the cards has got me into this fucking mess."

"That's why you must tell your side of the story. So, what did you do next?"

"I put the money and cards in my pockets and left. I ran down the corridor and came to the bodies again. I stepped over them as I was going to go to the next floor, but I couldn't. I couldn't breathe. So I went outside and sat down on the grass. I was looking around, watching what was going on and thinking of those dead bodies."

"What time was this?"

"Not sure. I guess about seven."

"When were you arrested?"

"As I was sitting on the grass, a copper shouted and started walking towards me. It was the same one I'd seen in the hotel. He grabbed my arm, took me to his car, searched me and that's when he found the bloody card and my passport. He checked the names and handcuffed me as soon as he saw they were different."

"What about the other one? You said that you took two cards?" Paul checked back on his notes.

Journalists...they don't miss a trick.

"I did, but he only searched my back pockets and I had the other one in my front, which I forgot about cos it happened so quickly. He handcuffed me and threw me in the back seat. That's when I remembered about the card and I stupidly hid it in a vent, but they found it and that's when the shit really hit the fan."

I stood up. I was a bit unsteady on my feet due to the whisky. I walked slowly across the room towards the door to the terrace. The door was closed and I gently placed my head against the double-glazed glass. With the sun reflecting on my face, I stared out at the far distant view of the sea.

"Paul, I know I screwed up with the cards, but I didn't start the fire, I swear. And that's what I'm charged for. It's fucking crazy and I just don't know what to do."

"I know you didn't. I believe you. But it's not me you have to convince, it's the court."

"Exactly. The court. What if I don't convince them?"

"I guess we'll have to cross that bridge when we come to it."

"Well, I'm hanging from that bridge now by my fucking neck. It's easy for you to say — it's me who's been charged."

I poured another drink and sat back down.

"That's why I need to print the truth, and I will." Paul closed his pad and stood up. "I need to go to the office. I'll see you later."

Before he left, he threw a packet of razors towards me that belonged to his German flat mate, Robert.

"Here. You need one hell of a shave; you'll look better for the court case. Robert won't mind."

"Thanks," I replied, catching the packet in my hands.

He also handed me a blanket.

The door closed and I heard Paul's fading footsteps along the corridor. I poured the last drop of the bottle into my glass, drank it, and with my head spinning, I lay back on the sofa.

Lost in thought, I focused on the rise and fall of the razor packet on my chest with each breath that I took. When my eyes began to get heavy, I pulled the blanket over my head to shut out the light, and for those few beautiful moments between awake and sleep, I was at peace. It was only when a door slammed somewhere in the apartment building that I jumped and my brain kicked back into action.

Dave, you've got to do something.

Chapter 16

GEORGE MICHAEL

Nine hours and nine razors later I felt the smooth skin of my face. I didn't look so bad after all, apart from the week old clothes I was wearing. I'd been up for an hour or so — since eight when Paul had woken me with a mug of coffee.

"I'll be at the office for most of the day, so hang onto the key," Paul said, picking up his wallet from the three legged antique table in the hallway, the one piece of furniture that seemed lost amongst the modern décor.

"Okay, thanks."

"See ya later," he said, closing the door behind him.

I walked straight to Paul's bedroom and opened the door. Seeing that my passport was still on the bedside table, I closed the door and went back to the kitchen.

My mind was working overtime as I tied my laces. I needed to phone home to talk with Dad and I wasn't looking forward to it in the slightest.

Wearing a blue baseball cap that I'd borrowed from Paul, I left the apartment, walked down the thirty eight steps and emerged in the bright morning sunshine. The cap had the standard white Nike tick on the front and wasn't something I'd normally choose to wear, but as it partially covered my face and was somewhat of a disguise it made me feel less paranoid.

Crossing the main road, I hurried along the cobblestone street until a few yards ahead of me I spotted a telephone box. I ran the last few feet, slid into the kiosk and picked up the receiver. Suddenly my mind was blank and I had no idea what to do; it seemed like an age ago when I'd called Mum from the hostel and I'd completely forgotten the procedure. It was the thought of Mum that made me change my mind about calling home; I really didn't feel ready to face her.

Scanning the board in front of me, my eyes flitted from top to bottom, ignoring the blur of Spanish until I finally found the English translation I was looking for.

'For operator services, please dial zero'.

Of course, you idiot!

In what seemed like an eternity but was just a few seconds, a female voice answered. "Can I help you?" she said, her broken English crackling down the line.

"Yes. I need to make a call to the UK and want to reverse the charges."

"To the UK?"

"Yes, yes please," I told her.

"And to which number?"

I gave her one of my brother's numbers: his office. He was also working in the property business just outside London in a leafy and wealthy area of Middlesex, as a manager for an established Estate Agency.

I waited impatiently listening to the whirrs and clicks on the end of the line. Finally he answered.

"Robert speaking. Can I help you?"

He always preferred to be called Robert at work; he thought it sounded more businesslike, but to me my youngest brother would always be Bob or Bobby.

"I have a collect call from Spain. Will you accept it, Sir?"

Christ, of course he'll fucking accept it I said under my breath.

When I heard the click of the operator leaving the call, I spoke.

"Bob, it's me."

"Dave...what the fuck's going on? Are you alright?

"I'm fine," I lied, slightly taken aback by his greeting.

"We've been reading about you."

"What?" My stomach flipped and I held the receiver closer to my ear.

"The papers," he went on. "You're in most of them. They're saying you're charged with theft and arson. That people have died. What the hell's happened?"

I hadn't looked at a paper for days, maybe a week, due to being holed up in the cell. Suddenly I felt uneasy. I looked to my left, then my right and tilted the baseball cap further forward to try and hide my face. A woman glanced at me as she passed and I turned my back on her, the paranoia consuming me.

"Bob, I never started the fire, I swear. I wasn't even there when it started. I saved two people's lives; I bet that's not fucking mentioned, is it?"

"No," he snapped. "It isn't." How the fucking hell did you get into this mess?"

I let out a huge sigh. "It's a long story. I'll tell you everything when I see you, I promise."

"Yeah, right," he retorted. "And when will that be exactly? You've been charged, Dave. The papers say the court case is already arranged."

"Well they've got something right then. It's the day after tomorrow. It's crazy, Bob, it really is. Everything's such a fucking mess and I don't know what the hell to do...I just can't..."

"Slow down, slow down. Where are you staying?"

"With this guy, Paul. He's a journalist. I'm staying with him until the hearing. I told him everything yesterday — exactly what happened — and he's gonna print my story. The real story."

"Well, let's hope he does bro. Mum's a complete mess. One minute she was doing the ironing and flicking through teletext and the next minute your name was all over the fucking screen, right in front of her."

"Shit."

Nobody said anything for a while; I just stood there with the phone against my ear and my head resting on the glass pane of the kiosk. All I could picture was the look on Mum's face after the drink driving charge: the look of disappointment. I felt ashamed.

Bob broke the silence.

"Guess what? In one of the papers, your story's right next to a photo of George Michael."

I laughed — we both did — but it was short-lived.

"Another one said you stole a fifty eight grand engagement ring from the hotel."

My eyes widened with the thought of it. "It's a lie, Bob. It all is." I paused, realising what I'd just said. "Well, most of it is, anyway. I did take some cash and a couple of credits cards... I'm guilty of that but..."

"Dave! You fucking idiot!"

"I know, I know. It was wrong and I hold my hands up to it, but I was desperate. I was messed up, Bob. So much has happened... stuff you haven't even read about. And seeing those fucking dead bodies..."

My voice slipped away as the images came back to haunt me. Bob didn't say a word and I wasn't sure what he was thinking. It unnerved me.

"I didn't have anything to do with the fire. Nothing. And that's what they're charging me with; arson and bloody manslaughter. But I didn't do it, I swear I didn't."

I don't know how long the silence lasted but I gripped the phone like my life depended on it.

"I believe you, Dave."

When I heard his words, the emotion I felt was immense. It was as if someone who'd been sitting on my chest for the past few days had suddenly decided to get off. I took the biggest breath I could and felt my lungs fill with the comfort of having someone on my side, someone who believed in me. Yes, Paul had been there for the past few days, but he didn't know me. His belief in me meant nothing.

"Anyway," I said, "how's Dad? I really need to speak to him. Is he okay?"

"He's pretty calm, actually. It's Mum who's angry and upset with you... disgracing our name and all that. She's not happy, Dave. Anyway, why do you need Dad?"

"I need a favour; a big one. And I can't ask Mum. Bob... take this number down, phone Dad and get him to call me now, okay? I'll be waiting. I'm in a phone box, so be quick."

I could hear him opening and closing a drawer. "What's the number?"

I carefully read it out to him, two digits at a time, and made him repeat it back to me.

"Just look after yourself, for God's sake. We're so worried, and Mum... well..."

His voice trailed off.

"Don't, Bob. I know. You don't have to tell me."

"Dave, just...I don't know... just take care, alright? I love ya, mate."

I swallowed the lump in my throat. "I love you too, Bob."

I put the phone back on the hook and stood there for a while, tapping my fingers against the window pane, pulling myself together and waiting for it to ring.

It didn't ring.

Did I give him the right number? I started to doubt myself as the seconds turned to minutes and the minutes — it seemed — were turning to hours. I paced around outside, back and forth, kicking my feet over the loose cobblestones on the ground. I collected a handful and tried to place them in a pyramid on the verge. It was trickier than I'd anticipated — the ground was uneven due to a clump of dried up weeds. I pulled a few out, brushed at the loose dirt with my fingers to flatten the earth and tried again, successfully this time. With another small stone I knocked the pyramid down, a stone at a time, and then rebuilt it.

I began to think my Dad wasn't calling.

'If I knock off the top grey stone, the phone will ring within the next ten seconds.'

Bloody mind games.

I dislodged the stone on my first attempt and it fell amongst a couple of fag butts and an ice lolly stick. I picked it up.

Staring at the phone and tossing the stone from one hand to another, I began to count: One, two... come on Dad, hurry up... six seven... please, just get on the fucking phone... and then just on cue, on number ten, it rang. I darted to the kiosk and had the receiver in my hand before the second ring.

"Dad?"

"Yes Dave, it's me."

"Look... I know I've screwed up again, but I really need you to help me."

"For Christ sake, why is it always bloody you? Your Mum's so upset and angry. She cried so much when she read the papers. Dave, everyone is so worried."

He was calm, just like Bob said, and it took me by surprise.

"I'm so sorry. But I didn't start the fire, I swear I didn't. Dad, it's me... you know I'd never do anything like that."

"I know, son. We all do. But you've been charged with it. This is bloody serious."

"Tell me about it."

I heard him take a deep intake of breath and blow it out slowly.

"How are you?"

"I've just spent a week in a cell with nothing to eat apart from bloody oranges. I've got no clothes... everything's gone... apart from what I'm wearing. Dad, I need to get out of here. I can't handle it. I need a ticket from Malaga airport... I don't give a shit where to... just book me a flight, please Dad."

He didn't say anything but I could hear him pacing up and down, his slippers clicking across the floor.

"Dad?"

"Son, it's wrong."

My Dad was an honest, hardworking man. I knew what I was asking him to do would be going against everything he believed in.

"I know it's wrong. But I can't deal with this. They could put me in prison, Dad. Fucking prison! I can't do it. . . I just can't. . . .please. . . book me a ticket, please. . . "

There was a pause. I closed my eyes really tightly and started to see patterns, binary and grids. I held my breath. Then Dad spoke.

"So they didn't take your passport?"

"Yes, they did. But I've got it. Well. . . I can get it."

"David. . . "

"Dad, please. . . no questions. . . just help me. . . please help me. . . "

His voice was low and I could hear all the hurt in it as he said a single word: "Okay."

There was a pause and I breathed out a huge sigh of relief.

"I need to get out of here tomorrow. The court case starts the day after. I'll pay you back for this, I swear."

"I'll make some calls and see what I can do. I'll phone you later. Can I call on this number?"

"Yes. Say about six?"

"Okay. Speak then, son."

"Thanks Dad, I love y. . . "

Before I could finish, the line went dead.

The sun was at its strongest at that time of day and for once the heat didn't agree with me. I needed some shade, so with a quick pace to my stride and looking down to count the cobblestones, I made my way back to Paul's apartment. I turned the key, opened the door and heard someone in the kitchen. I closed the door quietly.

"Shit." I blurted out loud, taking a step back as a man appeared in the hallway.

"Are you the English one who used all my razors?" he asked, his distinctive accent telling me he was the German flat mate.

I wanted to say: are you the German one whose razors they were? But I thought better of it as I'd used the whole packet.

"Yes, I am," I said. "Paul gave them to me. He said you wouldn't mind."

"Well I fucking do."

"Sorry," I shouted as he passed me, strode to his bedroom and slammed the door.

I also headed for a bedroom — Paul's. I opened the door carefully so not to disturb Robert and a smile appeared on my face when I saw my passport was still on the bedside table.

"Just be there tomorrow... just be there," I prayed under my breath.

The hands on the square-shaped clock in the kitchen ticked their way to five forty five. I finished my fourth coffee in as many hours, put the baseball cap back on and made my way out of the apartment. I ran to the telephone box and waited for Dad's call.

Please God, let him have a ticket. Please...

I repeated the words like a mantra, over and over again, until finally the phone rang. I picked up the receiver and held it against my ear.

"Dad?"

"Yes Dave. Good news. I phoned around and managed to get a flight, tomorrow night at seven into Gatwick."

I thought my heart was going to leap out of my chest. "That's fantastic! Thanks Dad!" I started to shake, the enormity of what I was about to do suddenly registering with me. "So, where do I get the ticket?"

"You have to go to a travel agent in Fuengirola. It was the only way to get you a flight at short notice. I've got the address..."

"That's fine... really Dad... I can't believe I'm coming home! Okay, hold on, two seconds, I need to get a pen."

There was nothing in the phone box and the closest building was a cafe across the road. I let the phone hang, swinging back and forth like a pendulum, and trying to keep my eye on it in case someone picked it up I dashed over the road, picked up an old receipt from a table and practically snatched a pen from the waiter.

"I'll bring it right back," I yelled, darting back across the road.

"Okay Dad, what's the address?"

I wrote down the details, double checked them and thanked him again for his help.

"Just get there and get on that plane. I'll be at the airport to pick you up, okay?"

I nodded my head, unable to speak.

"I'll see you tomorrow, son."

When I heard the click of the receiver I hung up the phone. In just over twenty four hours, I'd be going home.

On my way back to the apartment there was just one thing on my mind — one thing standing between me and my freedom.

I had to get my hands on that passport.

Chapter 17

MISERY

The apartment was as quiet as I'd left it and both Paul and Robert were out. I placed the baseball cap where I'd found it — hanging from a hook above the lonely three legged table in the hallway — and walked to Paul's bedroom. I hesitated outside and tapped on the door, just to make sure. As I expected there was nothing but silence.

The passport was still in exactly the same place. Even though I could see it clearly from the doorway, I walked over to the bedside table and picked it up, checking the photo to make sure. The same face staring back at me confirmed it was mine.

Do I take it now? Or wait till the morning when Paul has left for work?

But if he takes it with him, I'm fucked.

And If I take it now, he'll see that it's missing. And I'm fucked.

I heard someone fumbling with a key, trying to unlock the apartment door.

What are you gonna do, Dave?

The apartment door opened and I heard footsteps in the hall.

"Shit", I muttered, placing the passport back in exactly the same spot. I tiptoed back out of the room, closed the door and headed quickly over to the bathroom directly opposite. Within seconds of closing the bathroom door, the footsteps passed and carried on towards the kitchen. I needed to pee anyway and I took care of it with my hands trembling and beads of sweat pricking at my face. I flushed the toilet, swilled my hands under the tap and wiped them on a towel, running it over my forehead before putting it back.

Paul was on the terrace and leaning against the black wrought iron rail. He turned around when he heard me.

"Hi Dave. How're ya doin'?"

"I'm good, thanks. I was in the bathroom."

He gave a flick of his head as if to say ' right...okay' and I cursed myself for being such an idiot. What the fuck did you say that for? Where else would you have been?

I joined him on the terrace. The view was majestic: the lush green gardens complimenting the blue of the cloudless sky with the calm, sparkling sea in the distance.

"Fancy a cold beer?"

"Sure, don't mind if I do. Thanks."

Returning from the kitchen he handed me an open bottle. I took a mouthful. I needed it.

"You look edgy," he said, picking away at the San Miguel label on the bottle.

"And so would you if you were up in court."

He nodded. "How are you feeling about it?"

"Oh, I can't wait, you know, being accused of something I didn't do."

"I'd said I'll be there to help you."

"And what happens if you can't?"

"Well, we'll cross that bridge when we ...."

"Come to it. Yeah, yeah... but it'll be too fucking late then, won't it?" I went inside and sat on the sofa. Paul followed me in.

"Fancy another?" he said, heading for the fridge.

I nodded.

He handed me the bottle and went back out on to the terrace.

Sipping my beer, I stood up walked over to the book shelf that was free standing against the back wall. Eyeing my way across the hardbacks, something caught my attention: a thin booklet entitled Costa Del Sol. I put the bottle on the top shelf and slid it out. Flicking through the pages, I passed the typical tourist information jargon until I reached what I hoped would be there: maps of the local area.

"You alright mate? You coming out here?" Paul shouted from the terrace.

"Yeah, sure. Just having a look at your books," I said as I searched the index at the back for Fuengirola.

"There's a great selection. Help yourself," he replied.

Flipping to the map on page nine, I saw the coast line to the right — a beautiful, vast expanse of blue. Next to it was a selection of green, blue and purple colour coded roads. I knew where I was and I knew where I needed to be and my eyes carved out the route on the page. Motorways and streets, A355, A355-7, A7102, turn left here, turn right there, over this roundabout, over the next roundabout: it went on for miles and miles. Looking at the index beside the map it told me the journey was about thirty five miles, beginning to end.

"Found one you like yet?"

Fingering the different coloured spines of the neatly stacked books on the top shelf, I paused at a title: Misery. Sounds about right, I said under my breath. It was sandwiched between The Tommy Knockers and Christine. I pulled the book out, opened it and hid the map between the pages.

"Yep, Misery."

"Oh that one! It's a great book; I'm a big fan of Stephen King."

I wouldn't have guessed.

"I can see! I'll check it out tonight."

I joined Paul back out on the terrace where he was reclining on a sun lounger and basking in the late evening sun.

"By the way, I'm out tonight; a bloody work meeting. I'll be out most of the day tomorrow too, so I'll catch up with you tomorrow night, okay?"

"Yeah, fine," I said. But just don't take the bloody passport, I heard myself thinking.

Paul headed indoors and I sat on the terrace enjoying the rest of my beer, taking in the last remains of heat from the day's end. I focused on a bird as she flew higher and higher into the sky, her wings a perfect silhouette against the withering sunlight. This time tomorrow night, I thought, as she became nothing more than a dot in the sky, I could be on my way home.

Chapter 18

QUESTIONS

"Help yourself to another beer and something to eat, Dave. There's a lot to talk about before court, so I'll see you tomorrow."

"Okay, thanks Paul," I shouted into the hallway. "And yeah, we'll definitely chat tomorrow." I opened the fridge under the kitchen worktop, pulled a cold one from the row of bottles lined up on the shelf and flipped the top off with an opener. "Actually, I've got other plans," I said out loud when I heard the door close.

Taking a sip of beer, I scanned the contents of the fridge and grabbed four slices of ham, four slices of white bread and a jar of mayonnaise, immediately thinking of the son of Elvis as I made my sandwiches. I wondered where he was; how he was. I wondered what his life had been like and how many more stories he could have told me had I stuck around a bit longer. It was ironic to think that had I hung out with a homeless, drug-taking bum on the beach, I wouldn't have even been in this mess.

Picking up Misery along with my food and beer, I headed out to the terrace and lay back on the lounger. The night sky looked beautiful and I was mesmerised for a while by the stars twinkling against the blackness with nothing but a gentle murmur of people below and the distant sound of the swishing sea in the distance. Across the horizon, tiny lights bobbed up and down from the ships castaway in the emptiness of the ocean. The night was still humid but there was a slight breeze which, when caught, made my whole body shiver.

I opened the book and the map slipped out onto my lap. Twenty odd miles to Fuengirola and another fifteen or so to Malaga airport. It looked like a simple, straight forward route on the map, but that wasn't the problem; the problem was how the hell would I get there with no money or transport? I guessed hitch hiking and walking were my only two choices. And this was my choice; no one else's. I was scared — in fact I was terrified — of the consequences of court, the chance of being found guilty and then the eventuality of prison. There wasn't any way I could handle what all of that would entail so I had no choice but to leave. But I was equally as petrified at the prospect of running.

My thoughts turned to my family and all I was putting them through; how I was embarrassing them and shaming our name. I felt terrible for bringing my Mum to her knees and I felt terrible about asking Dad to buy a ticket and for putting him in that position.

"I'll sort your ticket out Dave, but it's wrong. You know that. You're jumping bail and you'll be in serious trouble with the law if you get caught. But you're innocent, son. You are innocent, aren't you? So it will be okay, won't it?"

It was a question I couldn't answer and nor could he. Quite frankly, I didn't want to face it.

I knew deep down that Dad was right — that what I was about to do was wrong on so many levels — but I couldn't take the chance of the alternative. It would be their word against mine. Who would the judge be more likely to believe? Me, a homeless, broke Englishman who'd been found with stolen credit cards at the scene of the crime, or the Spanish police who were so convinced I was guilty that they were taking me to trial? Even though I was grateful for Paul's offer of help, he was no lawyer. What the hell could a British journalist with no legal experience possibly achieve in a Spanish court room? What could he possibly do or say to get me off?

The more I thought about it, the more convinced I became that

they'd find me guilty. But the more I thought about running —
fleeing, jumping bail, whatever one would call it — the more panicky
I became. Dave, you can't run. What happens if you get caught?
You'll be fucked. If you think it's serious now, just you wait. They'll
lock you up for life.

Every bone in my body was telling me to run. But if I did, I
knew the next twenty four hours would be the most dangerous and
terrifying of my life. The questions continued. What if you don't
make it to the airport in time? What if they arrest you at the travel
agents? What if you don't make it through passport control? What
if Paul notices the passport missing and calls the police? They'll shut
down every fucking border out of this place.

A trickle of sweat made its way down on to the tip of my nose
and I wiped it away with the back of my hand. That's not sweat,
Dave. . . it's a fucking tear! How the hell do you expect to pull this
off when you can't even hold yourself together?

I stood up and paced the balcony, unable to settle. My mind was
a muddle of questions for which I had no answers. I tried to think of
another time in my life where I had to make a decision — a serious
decision — when I had absolutely no idea what to do. I drew a
complete blank.

The moon was full — a huge white orb in the sky — and it shone
down in all its glory, highlighting the curves of the waves. I leant
against the balcony rail watching the glimmering lights of the sea
rising and falling, with the mash of thoughts in my head becoming
nothing but a jumbled mess. When a sudden gust of wind took me by
surprise, a cold shiver played tag along my spine. I tried to convince
myself it was just the weather but I wondered if somebody somewhere was trying to tell me something. My muscles tightened and
my stomach felt like a brick as reality took its hold of me. I had to
make a decision — quickly — and stick to it. Faltering at this point,
with so little time left, was doing me and my nerves no favours at all.

The night drew on and the moon slid further across the sky, but
my mind hadn't settled. With fear lapping in my belly, I slipped into

the lounge, walked through the hallway from the kitchen and headed for Paul's room. His door was partially open and again I hesitated, tapping on the door. My passport — covered with a slight layer of dust — was still there. It hadn't moved, not even a centimeter from its spot on the bedside table.

Do I take it now?

Will he notice?

Of course he will, you fucking idiot.

I knew if I was going to do this, I had to wait till the morning. "Just another few hours", I heard myself say as I felt the alcohol from my fifth bottle of San Miguel take another stab at my ever-growing, unstable mind.

Leaving the bedroom door as I found it, I headed back to the terrace. I clocked a packet of Marlboro cigarettes on the side table in the living room and picked it up along with the box of swan vestas sitting on top of it.

Outside the night was still humid but there was a cold chill in the air. I struck the match against the side of the box and sheltering it with my hand I lit the cigarette and inhaled. My first drag felt pretty heavy on my head and made me slightly dizzy but I became seduced by the fragrance of the smoke and inhaled again. As I exhaled I watched with fascination the small circles of smoke rings I blew, each one growing larger, spiraling upwards and eventually evaporating into the darkening sky.

With each intake of smoke, my breathing quickened. I sat down on the lounger and with the anticipation of the next twenty four hours nursing me, put my face in my hands. My shoulders convulsed, releasing all the tension I'd felt over the past seven days.

I knew I had to do what I had to do. But always at the back of my mind, haunting me, there was a single thought.

If I run, will I make it?

Will I make it back home?

Chapter 19

HEADLINES

Particles of dust floated lazily around the living room as the morning sunlight streamed through the double-glazed doors. I'd been awake for an hour or so, unable to think of anything but the day ahead. Although my mind was perfectly clear and I knew exactly what I had to do, I couldn't settle; my stomach was in twisted knots. I walked through to the terrace, leaned over the balcony and gazed out at the calmness of the ocean in the distance, trying to block out the sound of Paul clattering noisily about in the kitchen.

"Hey Dave, there's a coffee on the table."

"Thanks," I said, not bothering to turn around.

Out at sea, a liner was making its way across the horizon, on its way to another place. I watched it inching its way across the water as if at any moment it would be sucked beneath the waves and lost forever.

"Right, I'm off to work. I'll be back around twelve," Paul said.

Did he just say twelve?

"There's a lot to talk about before tomorrow," he went on, "so we'll chat this afternoon, okay?"

I spun around to face him, my heart suddenly in my throat. "Twelve?" I said, trying to sound calm. "I thought you said you were working till seven."

"Change of plan. I think you need me a lot more than they do today."

I stood there, frozen to the spot, not having a clue what to say or do. Fuck. All the plotting... the phone calls... the hours I'd stared at the ceiling, meticulously planning everything down to the very last detail...and for what? For him to just fuck it all up?

I had to think of something, and fast. If Paul was going to be in the apartment all afternoon and expected me to be there, I needed a reason to not be. How the hell I was going to get hold of my passport without him noticing it was gone was another matter entirely, because the first thing he always did after work, without fail, was go to his room to get changed. Still, I had no time to worry about that yet.

"I've got plans this afternoon," I said, racking my brain for an excuse. "I'm sorry, mate. I didn't think you'd be here."

"Plans?" He looked at me, the slight tilt to his head unnerving me.

Shit. He's suspecting something already. Think Dave!

"Yeah," I said, suddenly conjuring up the man who'd been on my mind for the last few days. "The Son of Elvis; I bumped into him yesterday on the beach. We're meeting up for a walk and a smoke later...ya know, what with it being my last day of freedom."

"Will you stop being so bloody pessimistic. You don't know that."

"Okay," I said, relieved that he may have believed it. "I'll rephrase it. We're meeting up for a smoke later...ya know, what with me fucking shitting myself about court tomorrow."

For a moment we just stared at each other and nobody said a word. Then, with a shrug of his shoulders and a quick shake of his head that implied he wasn't at all happy about it, he said "fair enough" and picked up his jacket.

"When will you be back?" he said, standing in the doorway.

"Seven? Like we originally agreed?"

"How about six?" he said, picking up his keys.

"Fine," I told him, not wanting to argue with him or draw attention to my panic, even though I knew that just one single hour could bring about my downfall. "I'll see you at six."

Paul left the building and I stretched my body over the balcony, waiting until I saw him push open the main apartment doors and appear in the street. When he strolled to the end of it and turned the corner, I went back into the living room, picked up my coffee and checked the clock in the kitchen. The second hand ticked its way around it, sweeping past the numbers at an alarming speed. It was nine twenty and there were less than ten hours to go until my flight. I finished my coffee and balanced the mug strategically in the sink on top of the dirty plates from the night before. Heading towards Paul's bedroom and pumping with adrenaline, I suddenly heard a door slam shut.

"Shit, Robert," I said under my breath, completely forgetting he hadn't yet left for work.

"Guten Morgen," I said, facing him in the hallway. I'd picked up a German phrase or two in the last few days in an attempt to be civil towards him, but it hadn't worked so far. As expected, he completely ignored my greeting, stared at me as he passed me, and then left the apartment, slamming the door behind him.

Great... he's fucked off, the freak, I thought, taking the final steps to Paul's room. I had no idea why Robert hated me so much, but to be honest, I didn't give a shit.

Paul's door was closed. I knocked — as I always did — and unsurprisingly, no one answered. I turned the handle, pushed open the door and my eyes immediately steered towards the bedside table.

There, next to the lamp, was my passport.

I walked directly to the table and stared at it, my eyes flitting from the passport to the lamp and back again.

In my mind I was eight years old and back at home, sprawled out on the lounge floor with Pink. There'd be twenty items laid out on the carpet in front of us and I'd study each one before closing my eyes, waiting for Pink to take one of them and hide it away. We used Mum's egg-timer to count down the seconds — I was only allowed three minutes to tell her which item was missing. I usually told her in about fifteen seconds.

I picked up the passport, held it in my hand and stared at the table
— a table that now looked incomplete. I shifted the lamp, shoved it
more to the middle, trying to hide the empty space. It looked odd
and I moved it back again. I glanced around the room and saw a
book on the chest of drawers; Stephen King: The Running Man. I
grabbed it and carefully placed it in the empty space, first vertically
and then horizontally, shifting the angle until it looked right. But no
matter which way I turned it, it looked awkward.

I perched on the edge of the bed and stared at the floor. Yes, I
could take my passport and make my way to the airport, but Paul
would be back in his room by twelve fifteen, throwing off his trousers
and putting on his shorts. He'd notice it was gone; there was no two
ways about it — it would take a fucking tsunami to prevent him
getting out of his work clothes.

Clenching my fists in anger and frustration, I leant over and
thumped the pillows, over and over again. I grabbed the top one
from the four spread across the top of the bed and laid it across my
lap, burying my head straight into the middle of it. My eyes closed,
my tears filling them. White squiggly lines floated under my eyelids,
dashing back and forth. I tried to rein in my thoughts; my mind
telling me that I had to think, to fight, but my heart telling me I'd
already lost.

You're not going home, Dave. Just face the music. It's over.

I must have stayed in that position for five minutes or so, feeling
like my whole world had collapsed around me. I needed my passport
and it was there — right there in front of me — but there was no
way I could take it. It was thirty five miles to the airport and Paul
would notice it gone and alert the police way before I'd made it even
a quarter of the way there.

I was fucked.

I sobbed — my tears dampening the clean, white cotton of his
pillowcase — knowing that the game was up. I could move that lamp
around the table as many times as I wanted, but the irregularity
would always be there, glaringly obvious with its passport shaped

space.

There's only one thing that looks like a passport, Dave. And that's a passport.

I sat bolt upright on the bed.

Dave, you're a fucking genius.

My heart thumped in my chest and I could feel small beads of sweat beginning to form on my forehead. I reached over to the bedside drawer below the lamp, yanked it open and rummaged through a stack of papers and envelopes, a couple of batteries and a condom. But there was no passport. I ran around the double bed to check the other bedside table that housed a digital clock and a matching lamp. Big red numbers displayed the time: nine thirty five. I closed my eyes, repeating under my breath, please be there, please be there. I opened the drawer and rummaged through it: another heap of papers, a couple of pens and a half empty tube of cream. I glanced at the label, not recognising the name, wondering what it was for, but threw it back down and carried on looking. There was still no passport.

I had to get to the travel agent to pick up that ticket. I had to get on that plane at seven o clock. I had to find it.

In fury, I slammed shut the drawer and the lamp toppled over, falling onto the floor. I bent down, picked it up and placed it in exactly the same position it had come from — with its base perfectly covering the only shape on the desk that was free of dust.

Patches of sweat appeared on my shirt under my arms as the heat suddenly became unbearable. I wasn't sure if it was me or the room and I glanced out of the window. The sun was getting higher in the sky and glancing back at the clock I saw nine thirty nine become nine forty. My breathing quickened; I had just over nine hours to get on that plane.

I knelt down and searched under the bed. Nothing; just shoes and empty boxes. Standing up, I walked towards the mahogany five drawer cabinet beneath the window. Wiping the sweat from my brow, I felt my blood pulsating around my body and rushing straight to my head, like a milkshake being sucked hard through a straw. I opened every drawer from top to bottom and then again from bottom to top, pushing around various items of clothing, tee shirts, shorts, jumpers, underwear and socks, but nothing.

To my left was the en-suite bathroom. I dashed in and opened the mirror fronted medicine cabinet above the wash hand basin. Facing me were a selection of small medicine bottles, a tube of toothpaste, some shaving foam and razors, but no passport.

He had razors, the bastard.

There was a brown, clear bottle with Paul's name clearly printed on the label: a bottle of pills for high blood pressure. I considered taking a couple but thought better of it. I closed the cabinet door and caught my reflection staring back at me. Even though I was clean shaven, total panic was etched across my face; I looked like I'd aged twenty years in twenty minutes.

Striding out of the bathroom I closed the door and slumped back down on the edge of the bed with one question replaying itself over and over inside my head: Where the fuck is it? C'mon Dave, where the hell would you keep yours if you lived here?

I stood up, steadied myself, placed the pillow back at the head of the bed and smoothed the creases on the duvet. Clocking the time on the other bedside table — nine forty five — I dashed out of Paul's room and headed for the lounge.

I stood in front of the bookcase — the bookcase I'd stood at just the day before where I'd found the map. Five wide shelves were crammed from left to right with paperbacks and hardbacks, with only the occasional ornament breaking up the monotony. I crouched down to the bottom shelf, placing my hands around a carved, wooden box on the left. Paul had slid it out a just few days earlier on our return from court, placing a bunch of stuff inside it. I hadn't taken much notice at the time — it was the farthest thing from my mind as I'd sat on his sofa, my mind reeling from the day's events. But now it was glaringly obvious — he'd pulled it out to store away some documents.

Sliding out the box and crouching to my knees, I placed it on the floor. There was a solid lid, held down by two hefty hinges, and I eased it open. The first thing I saw was his driving license, its corners squashed into every corner of the box. I dug it out and put it face down on the floor in front of me, turning my attention to what else lay inside. There were some folded pieces of paper, a building society logbook, a birth certificate, a cheque book and a set of keys.

No passport.

I shoved everything back in the order that I'd found it, squashing the driving license on top and into the corners of the box. I closed the lid and placed it back onto the shelf.

Bastard. Where the fuck is it?

I glanced around the room, my eyes flitting from floor to ceiling. It was sparsely decorated, most of the storage being in the kitchen — wall to wall cupboards that stored nothing but cutlery and crockery. There were two drawers on either side of the TV cabinet and I delved through them, finding nothing but a few video tapes, a sheet of stickers and an old TV remote. I'd already ploughed through his bedroom and bathroom and there was nothing else to check. I paced aimlessly around the room, my heart beating faster with every step I took.

You've missed something, Dave. You must have. Start again... and calm down.

I walked from room to room, methodically studying each surface, each piece of furniture, each shelf and every drawer. I felt like a policeman looking for fingerprints. Nothing. The only room I hadn't checked was Robert's and I stood in the hallway outside his door and contemplated it.

Why the hell would Paul's passport be in Robert's room, you idiot?

Even though I knew it was a long shot, I still had my hand on the door knob, ready to go in. I turned it, but hesitated, looking down the hallway to the main apartment door. The last thing I wanted was for Robert to find me in his room and although I knew he'd already left for work, I had an image of him waltzing back into the apartment and catching me knee deep in his belongings. I ran to the end of the hallway, checked the door was firmly closed and fastened the latch. As I turned to go back, I knocked my thigh against Paul's stupid, three legged table.

"Fucking hell," I said out loud, glaring at it and rubbing my leg.

And that's when I noticed the small brass knob — a knob that was attached to a very slim drawer.

For a moment I was stunned: I couldn't believe I hadn't noticed it before. I'd walked past it at least five times and had looked at it many more times than that. Christ, I'd even had a five minute discussion with Paul about where he'd got it from.

I slowly slid open the drawer with my heart almost skipping a beat and looked down at the only four items that were in there: a residence card, a health insurance certificate, a pair of sunglasses and a passport.

Snatching it up in my hand, I laughed out loud, the excitement and relief bubbling up inside of me. I closed the drawer with a smile firmly etched on my face and headed straight back to Paul's room. Stuffing my own passport into the back pocket of my jeans, I filled the empty space on the table with his. Squaring it up, I stood back and studied it.

It looked fucking perfect.

Before I left, I gave everything a once over — checking for creases in the duvet, straightening the pillows, pulling the door to the en-suite to just a couple of inches of being closed. I backed out of the room giving it all a final glance and shut the door behind me.

Back in the lounge, I pulled out the book Misery from the bookcase and opened it up. The map fell onto the floor and I bent down to pick it up before squeezing the book back into its slot. In the kitchen, I swilled out an empty orange juice carton and filled it to the brim with cold water from the half-gallon plastic container on the floor. Doubting myself, I checked my back pocket again for my passport and then reached into my front one, pulling out the crumpled receipt with the travel agent's address on it. Carefully unfolding it, I checked to make sure the words hadn't miraculously vanished overnight and then I folded it back up and slid it back into my pocket.

That was it. I had everything I needed and I was ready — or at least as ready as I'd ever be. There was a long journey ahead of me and with no money I knew, unless I was lucky, that it would be all on foot.

I went to the bathroom with the intention of taking a pee, but as much as I tried, I couldn't go. My body was in a state of panic, unwilling to co-operate with me. I tried to force myself but zipped myself up, taking a final look at myself in the mirror. With a map in one hand and a carton of water in the other, the person that stared back at me looked like a fucking convict. I pictured myself strolling into the airport without a single possession to my name other than the ticket I'd hopefully be holding in my hand.

A bag, Dave. You need a bag.

For the second time in just a few minutes, I found myself at Robert's door but this time there was no hesitation — I turned the handle and walked in. My jaw dropped immediately, nearly hitting the dusty marble tiles below. The smell of body odour was disgusting. Clothes were strewn across the floor, scattered amongst piles and piles of shoes, and the wardrobe opposite me was open, with the door hanging precariously from just the top hinge. Inside were a couple of lonely shirts, hanging from the rail.

Looking around the room, something caught my eye, and it wasn't just the unmade single bed with its soiled brown and cream striped duvet cover: it was the black and white newspaper clippings neatly placed in three rows on his two white pillows. Stepping over piles of dirty clothing, I walked over to the bed and standing next to a filthy, black laminate bedside table, my eyes were immediately drawn to the headlines of the clippings. I leant over to take a closer look and flinched, the shock of seeing my name in print shaking my entire body.

Scanning the words of one of the articles, I perched myself on the edge of Robert's bed. Bob had told me about this one and had even read it to me over the phone — the one that said I'd stolen a fifty eight thousand pound ring and that I'd been arrested for theft, arson and manslaughter. But seeing it in there in black and white completely threw me.

I started to tremble and took a deep breath in an attempt to control my breathing. I didn't want to see this stuff and I felt sick, the rancid smell of the room adding to my nausea, but my eyes flitted across the remaining cuttings on the bed and there, in bold, black letters was the headline:

I STEPPED OVER DEAD BODIES TO LOOT.

My stomach churned. Bob didn't mention this one to me. I sat there and read the story from beginning to end: about how I was in the hotel... how I saw dead bodies and stepped over them to steal cash and credit cards. There was nothing about saving lives, NOTHING. I read the article twice, maybe three times, trying to take it all in. And then I noticed the name of the journalist, printed just to the right of the story.

It was Paul.

"You fucking bastard," I said, emphasizing every syllable though gritted teeth.

"You sad, fucking bastard."

But why would he do that? Why? Yet another question I asked myself for which I had no answer.

Confused and emotional, the realization hit me: there wasn't anyone here who'd ever been on my side and as much as he'd tried to convince me, Paul had only been out for himself. The last remaining guilty thoughts I'd had about leaving — about leaving Paul to face that courtroom and the police without me — just disappeared. I had to get out of there and for the first time since I'd considered running I finally knew, right or wrong, that it was the only thing to do.

I stood up, left the paper clippings as I'd found them, made my way out of the room and closed the door. At the end of the hallway I reached up, took the baseball cap off the hook, looked into the mirror and put it on, tilting it forwards to partially cover my eyes. My heart was beating fast and I swallowed hard, took a deep breath and spoke to the face reflecting back at me.

"Dave, you can do this."

I tossed the apartment keys onto the three legged table, released the latch on the door and walked out.

I was inches away from closing the door, inches away from leaving the apartment for the very last time, when two things suddenly hit me. I pushed open the door and ran back inside.

Heading back to Robert's room, I grabbed a rucksack from the floor, emptying out a few of his belongings onto an already substantial pile. Then I walked back to the three legged table and picked up the keys I'd left there just a few seconds before. I couldn't believe I'd been so stupid — if Paul had seen them it would have been a pretty convincing clue that I had no intention of returning.

I threw the map and water into the rucksack along with the keys and fastened it up. On a final whim, I took the sunglasses from the drawer and put them on. Without a second look back, I slammed shut the door and ran down the steps to the street outside.

The heat hit me with a vengeance. With the rucksack firmly strapped to my back, I took my first steps out of Marbella and along the street to Fuengirola. There were thirty five miles and eight and a half hours to go until the plane would leave the runway. I did the maths, turned the corner and quickened my step. I couldn't afford to get this wrong; there would be no second chance.

Striding along the main road and heading east along the seafront, I tightened the straps around my waist.

You can do this, Dave... you can...

I adjusted my sunglasses, tilted my cap and carried on walking, counting each and every paving slab beneath my feet. People passed me but I ignored them, keeping my eyes firmly fixed to the ground.

The rucksack was light, but the weight on my shoulders felt immense. If I'd stopped to think about it — really think about it — I don't think I'd have been able to do it. But my only thoughts were of Mum and Dad, my brothers and sister, and of stepping off that plane at Gatwick and feeling my home beneath my feet.

Chapter 20

THE RUSTY NISSAN

Sweat dripped slowly from under my cap and down onto my forehead as every step, every stride in the ever growing heat took it out of me. I marched along the street at a steady rate, eyes down, only occasionally glancing to my side to have a last lingering look at the ocean. Wanting to pace myself, I wondered how many miles I could walk in an hour but I had no idea. It occurred to me how much of a lazy bastard I'd been back in London, using the car at every available opportunity. For a moment I despised myself and made a promise to change things when I got home... if I ever got home.

As I made my way down the main road and out of Marbella, I tried my luck at hitching by the roadside, stopping every so often to face the cars coming towards me. But it was pointless. Drivers passed me by without even a look, their eyes staring straight ahead, unflinching. I carried on determinedly for a mile or so, only stopping when I reached a signpost on the pavement telling me there was a petrol station just fifty metres away, down a narrow side road to my right. I practically ran down it, hopeful that I'd find someone going my way, but the place was deserted. The station — if one could call it that — wasn't just closed but boarded up, and there wasn't a car or a person in sight. I stared at the old graffiti covered walls, the smashed in windows, and headed back up the hill.

Back on the main road I continued my journey with my arm outstretched and my thumb upright, praying for somebody to stop, but I
may as well have been invisible. Eventually I became bored of counting my footsteps, tired of watching the creases on the top of my
trainers fold and stretch, and so I raised my head to watch the traffic
go by. There was a steady stream of common cars — Polos, Nissans,
nothing out of the ordinary: cars I'd see every day on the streets
of London — but they were interspersed at an absurd ratio with
BMWs, Mercedes and Porsches, the sheen of their metal gleaming
flawlessly beneath the blistering sun. That's when it hit me that
Marbella really was a city for the rich and the corrupt... and that
was the moment I told myself that I couldn't wait to leave the place.
For the first time since I'd set off, I wondered about people's reactions
to hitchhikers in Marbella and whether I'd be lucky enough to get a
lift at all. Everyone seemed to be going about their business without
a thought of what was going on around them. They were people on
a mission — as I was — people who obviously had no intention of
allowing a solitary figure on the side of the road to intervene with
their plans, whatever they were. It certainly knocked my optimism
as I thought of the miles ahead of me, but it didn't knock my spirit:
I knew that if I had to travel the entire way on foot then I would,
even if it fucking killed me.

With every onward step, I thought about the time I'd spent there
— meeting the brothers Kelvin and Anthony, the lovely night I'd
spent with Emma, my time on the beach with the crazy son of Elvis
and his silly dog and, of course, the moments I'd spent with the beautiful Rosa, but those thoughts were soon overshadowed by images of
the hotel fire. Horrific pictures of the three dead bodies filled my
head, haunting me... their rigid, burnt faces staring vacantly into
space, their features grotesquely distorted. When I tried to shake
them off they were replaced with less disturbing images of my days
in the police cell, but it did little to calm me.

"Fuck" I said out loud, shaking, as I pounded the streets. I felt
unable to make sense of everything I'd been through and how the

hell it had all happened. I knew it wasn't over, not by any means —
I still had to get my ticket and get on that plane. Although I was
confident I'd get to Fuengirola and that my feet wouldn't give up
on me, I was absolutely terrified of getting caught. As I trudged on,
blisters forming on the soles of my feet, I knew there was a very real
possibility that things could go horribly wrong and that I wouldn't
even get to see the tarmac on the runway.

All it'll take is one person to recognize your name, Dave... just
one single person...

The cars sped past me in a monotonous trail as I marched the pavements like a copper on the beat on a London inner street. Thumbing
my way, praying for a lift, and doing all I could to prevent the images
from re-entering my mind, I played snooker with the cars; a game I
used to play years before. I awarded myself one point for spotting a
red car, two for a yellow and three for a green. At one point I had a
score of twenty-four, but then there was a sudden break in the traffic
and I was left staring disappointingly at an empty road. Twenty four;
it was a total I'd never even achieved on a snooker table when playing
with my mates back home in the pubs and clubs I used to frequent.
Snooker wasn't my game. If anything, I was a pool player, although
I wasn't particularly successful at that either. I had my lucky days
when I'd clear the table, but there were many more when I'd make
a complete ass off myself.

"You need to think ahead, Dave," my mates would laugh as I'd pot
an easy ball and suddenly realise I had nowhere left to go.

The irony of it sat in my stomach.

When the traffic picked up I reached out my arm again, half-
heartedly now as it was aching from having it horizontal for so long.
A shiny black Porsche roared on by, followed by a couple of Volvos
and a Citroen. "Stop, you bastards", I said out loud, as I watched
them disappear. And then there was a siren in the distance. It was
faint at first, creeping up on me, and I pulled my arm to my side,
lowering my head. I tilted my cap, adjusted my glasses and did all I
could to shrink myself, wanting more than anything to be as invisible

as I had been for the last couple of hours. I held my breath as the
noise of the siren cut through the air like a knife and I stuffed my
hands in my pockets as the sound grew louder and louder behind me.
I panicked, feeling my heart beating wildly in my chest.

Please God... no... don't stop.

The whirl of the siren magnified. I could feel the sound of the
engine against my back, closing in on me. I screwed my eyes up tight
but carried on walking and then, in an instant, felt the heat of the car
pass me. Without stopping, it slowly faded away and disappeared.

For the first time in miles, I stopped, reached round to the rucksack
on my back, unzipped a pocket and grabbed the carton of water.
Grasping it tightly in my hands, I swallowed two huge, luke-warm
mouthfuls, one after the other. Sweat dripped from my face and my
shirt clung to my back. It must have been approaching eighty degrees
and I was struggling, but I replaced the carton knowing I still had a
long way to go. Unzipping another pocket, I grabbed the map and
opened it up, looking at the places I'd already passed. Glancing up,
I saw a signpost for Santa Clara Golf Club and located it on the
map. Measuring the distance with my thumb and finger, and with a
determined boost of confidence, I carried on walking.

Not long after, I noticed a good looking and well- dressed couple
walking towards me — the only people I'd seen on foot since I'd
left Marbella town. I quickly adjusted my cap, pushed the sunglasses
firmly onto my nose, and when we were side by side I casually asked
them if they had the time, trying my best to not appear as nervous
as I felt.

"Sure!" the man said, unclasping his hand from his girlfriends and
easing up his shirt cuff. He looked down at his Rolex. "It's almost
midday."

"Thanks," I said, hurrying on, calculating that I'd walked about five
miles in ninety minutes. If I continued at the same speed, I'd reach
the travel agents by half past four and that wasn't even accounting
for me inevitably slowing down in the unbearable, afternoon heat
that I knew I'd have to face.

"Come on Dave," you can do this," I said out loud, marching ahead on what seemed to be a never-ending road. I had to move — and move fast — to stand any chance of reaching the airport and getting on that plane.

Keeping the map firmly in my hand I continued to walk along the A-7 with my left arm stretched out and my thumb pointing upwards, but it became increasingly difficult. The pavement narrowed and disappeared, giving way to a thin strip of wasteland. A barrier emerged, separating me from the roadside, and even though I continued to hold out my arm, I knew in my heart there was little chance of somebody stopping. Cars sped past me without even a hint of slowing down and my enthusiasm diminished fast as the ground became more uneven beneath my feet. As it was the coast road, I'd naively expected an ocean view for my journey, but it was not to be: it was an endless tree lined road with a backdrop of numerous hotels and businesses stretching on forever.

I passed through Alicate and then Costabella, Marbella's neighbouring villages, desperate to stop and rest. But there was no time. I needed a lift badly and for someone — anyone — to stop, but it seemed as though God was succeeding in inflicting his wrath on me.

I was miles away — in mind and in distance — when an old rusty Nissan van slowed down and pulled into a layby just ahead of me with thick black smoke billowing from its exhaust. Assuming the driver was in trouble, I expected him to get out of the car to check his engine, but he didn't move. It was only when I came up alongside him that he reached over the passenger seat, rolled down the window and spoke.

"Hey. Need a lift? Where ya goin'?"

At last!

"Fuengirola," I said, catching the distinct whiff of weed from the car. I looked into his eyes, bloodshot from the joint he held in his hand. He took a drag, held his breath for a few seconds and blew the smoke towards my face.

"Nope. Not goin' that far, man. Going to Ana Maria, a few miles up. Any good?"

Any good? It was brilliant.

"Fuck yes, thanks!" I said, with a smile stretching across my face.

He opened the door from the inside — surprisingly there was no handle on the outside — and I tossed my rucksack onto the floor. Throwing some oily rags from the passenger seat into the back of the car, I spotted some newspapers scattered on the back seat. For a moment I froze, wondering if he'd read the reports about me, but pulling myself together I climbed in, closed the door and unzipped the pocket of my rucksack for my water.

"Sorry 'bout the car," he said. "It needs a service but cash is a bit tight."

"I know the feeling," I told him.

"So where ya from man?" he asked, drawing on the joint that was hanging from his mouth.

Fucking questions I thought, but I felt obliged to answer. "London," I said without thinking, but then realised my mistake. Shit Dave, don't give too much away. "I've been here for a month, travelling, you know. Camping, sleeping on the beach. I'm just off to visit a friend in Fuengirola." As much as I wanted to tell him I'd been on a two week package holiday in a four star hotel, I was more than aware that I looked like I'd just finished a month long stint in Beirut.

"Cool. So what's your name?" he asked, passing me the last remains of the spliff.

Just make up a name... any name I thought.

"Steve," I said, and took a drag, feeling the sensation hit me almost immediately. "You?"

"Charlie. Been here for a couple of months. I'm on my way to see my girl... that's where I'll be dropping you off."

"That's great. Thanks for stopping, mate. I've been at it all morning."

"No worries Steve, no worries. I know what it's like." He tapped his fingers on the steering wheel to the beat of Reelin' in the Years that was crackling away on the radio, and I sat back wondering if I really did look like a Steve.

I adjusted my cap and sunglasses again and stared out of the passenger window for the rest of the journey. Hearing Charlie sing along to the music, he reminded me a little of the Son of Elvis; I guess it was the way he was so laid back. He had a great, chilled-out attitude. Actually, they both did.

Even in his old Nissan the journey flew past, and within about fifteen minutes we came to the junction where Charlie had to turn off for Ana Maria.

"This is it man, just carry on that way," he said, pointing to the right.

"Great, thanks." I said, reaching out to shake his hand.

"You'll get a lift easy man, but watch out. The cops don't like hikers round here, so keep an eye out."

Great, I thought. I opened the car door, grabbed the rucksack and got out, slinging it across my shoulder. "Are they that bad?"

"Yeah... they can be a fucking pain in the arse,"he said.

I nodded, knowing all too well.

"Hey, Charlie," I said before closing the door. "What time is it?"

He glanced down at his watch. "Quarter past one." His right eyebrow lifted. "Shit, I'm late," he said, revving the engine.

I smiled, slamming the door, and waved him off, watching as he sped down the side road with smoke pouring from the exhaust and Hotel California blaring from his speakers.

I strapped the rucksack firmly onto my back and checked that the receipt with the travel agent's address was still deep in my pocket before heading off along the road. Having walked just a few feet, a car sped past me, missing me by inches.

"Wanker!" I yelled, stepping over the curved face of the barrier and back onto the narrow strip of pavement.

With only my cap for shade and the blisters on my feet starting to sting, walking became difficult, but I kept going. I had no other choice.

After a mile or so the traffic became heavier and with every car, van and lorry that passed me, a gust of wind blew across the whole of my back before showering me with road grit. The wind was more than welcome; the grit not so much. I ambled along, counting my steps, my arm limp at my side but my thumb standing proud beneath the intolerable sun. Each time I sensed a vehicle approaching me I prayed that it wouldn't be a police car. You've come this far... don't fuck it up now, Dave, I told myself, plodding on with my head down.

My thoughts soon turned to home. I'd been so wrapped up in my own journey that it hadn't even occurred to me how my family might have been suffering. I gathered pace, thinking of Mum and Dad and all I'd put them through. With each step I took I thought of their anguish, of how they must have been feeling right at that moment, not knowing what the hell was happening to me and whether or not I'd make it back. Regardless of their disappointment in me, I knew that more than anything they'd want me safe at home and under the same roof. I walked on, wishing for the same, with my heart heavy in my chest.

Half a mile or so later and hearing a deep rumble behind me, I glanced over my shoulder to see a large truck approaching me. I turned my whole body around to face it and walking backwards, stretched out my arm and thumb, waving it frantically. Not for the first time, I began to talk to myself.

"Please stop, please God... let it stop."

I was mouthing the words over and over and to my relief it started to slow down.

"Come on... yes... just stop... please stop, for fuck's sake."

Honking his horn, the driver flashed his high beams and indicated right as I clenched my fist in triumph.

"Yes!" I shouted, turning around and stumbling over my own feet. I ran after the truck which had come to a halt a little way down the road. My heart was racing as I reached it, lifted myself onto the first step and opened the door.

With his beard and moustache covering most of his face and his black hair parted in the middle and touching his shoulders, the driver looked more Mexican than Spanish, but he certainly wasn't English.

"Fuengirola, por favor?" I asked, looking at him, my eyes wide in expectation.

"Si," he replied, nodding at me.

"Gracias."

I pulled off my rucksack, heaved my body up two further steps and grabbing the rail I flopped into the seat. As we set off, the first thing I did was search the dashboard for a clock. The time stared back at me in splendor: it was two twenty. I blew a heavy sigh of relief, let my head fall back onto the headrest and closed my eyes, mentally thanking Charlie for helping me. I had a couple of hours to get to the travel agents to collect my ticket and knowing I'd make it with plenty of time to spare, I allowed the elation — just for a moment — to take over.

Chapter 21

MANICURED NAILS

"Senor, senor."

Feeling a hand on my shoulder nudging me awake, I forced open my eyes and squinted against the bright sunlight flooding through the windscreen.

"Fuengirola, Senor."

"Sorry...yes, gracias."

Grabbing my belongings I opened the door, grasped the rail and jumped down onto the pavement, my mind still foggy with sleep. "Gracias," I mumbled again as I slammed shut the door and watched as the lorry weaved its way through the traffic, turned a corner and disappeared.

I let out a loud yawn, stretched my arms and searched through blurry eyes for a street name, pulling the receipt from my pocket to check the travel agent's address. Locating both points on the map, I saw that I didn't have far to go — just across the main square, past the church and down a few narrow streets. I put on my cap and glasses, pulled the rucksack onto my back and started to walk.

The people opposite me were forming an orderly queue at the station, waiting for the drivers of the yellow buses to slide open their doors and take them on their journeys. I passed them, curious as to where they were going, and then turned left, crossing a couple of small cobble-stoned streets. I envied them — these people — going about their day with nothing better to do than window shop, laze around in the sun and take fun trips to better places.

When the church bells chimed three times in the distance, a grin spread across my face; there were just four hours until my flight — four fucking hours until I'd be on my way home. "You can do this Dave," I told myself again. "You can do this."

The main square was heaving with people. Many were wandering around in the afternoon heat whilst others shaded themselves, drinking coffee and beer in the cafes and bars. I passed them with my head down, knowing that the remaining fifteen miles on foot without a drink was going to be tough. I thought perhaps I could ask for some water to fill my carton when I reached the travel agent but thought better of it, terrified I'd be drawing attention to myself. As I walked, the distance I still had to travel played heavily on my mind. Fifteen miles; I didn't need a mathematician to tell me that to stand any chance of getting my flight, I needed another lift. The elation I'd felt in the lorry vanished, and doubt that I'd make it there on time started to creep in. With every step I took I prayed — to God, to whoever was up there and listening to me — to get me to that airport.

When I came to the church, I glanced up at the clock on the stone-faced wall. It was three fifteen. My heart was thumping in my chest knowing I only had a few streets to go but time was running out. I quickly came to the second street, then the third and continued till I took a left at the fourth. The road was a cul-de-sac, most of it in shadow and obscured from the sun. Welcoming the shade, I propped myself against the wall and looked up to check the road sign, again taking the paper from my pocket just to make sure. "Yes!" I said, clenching my fist, so grateful that Dad had got it right. You're a fucking star, I told him in my head.

The left side of the street held nothing but a cafe, a bakery and a clothes shop, but right there, opposite the cafe, was a travel agent. Once more, I looked at the piece of paper, doubting myself, but deciding it was definitely the right place, I braced myself. Walking the few yards to the door, I grabbed my passport from my rucksack and took a deep breath.

This was it.

I pulled on the door handle but it didn't open. Perplexed, I pushed it. When it still didn't open I started to panic, rattling it back and forth in its hinges.

"Shit."

I hammered on the glass, but nothing. I checked the opening hours on the timetable that was hanging by a sucker on the door: nine am till six pm, Monday to Saturday. It was definitely Wednesday and it was the middle of the bloody afternoon.

"You should be fucking open!" I swore, pressing my face against the door. Shielding my eyes with my hands, I peered through the glass and saw nothing but darkness. The lights were off and there wasn't a person in sight.

"Shit, shit, shit," I shouted, kicking the concrete post next to me.

I glanced up and down the street looking for any sign of life, but it was deserted. Then, seeing two old women sitting inside the cafe next to the window, I ran across the road. Dashing through the door and ignoring them, I stopped at the counter. An elderly man, standing behind the till, was handing change to a young woman and talking to her in Spanish.

"Excuse me," I interrupted. "The travel agent...." I said, pointing towards the shop with my left hand, "...when will it be open?"

He looked at me, his lined face revealing nothing but a blank expression, and shaking his head he shrugged his shoulders. My heart was racing. I felt my shirt clinging to my already sweaty body and a single thought embedded itself in my mind: you're fucked.

But then the woman — the young, well-dressed, dark haired customer standing next to me — turned around. Eyeing me up and down distrustfully with her nose in the air, she said in near perfect English: "I work there, can I help you?"

I almost hugged her. Trembling with nervous excitement, I said, "My father booked a flight for me to Gatwick for tonight. He gave me your name and address to pick up the ticket."

She looked me up and down again, her face cold, and then shoved her change into her brown leather purse. "Okay, follow me, please," she finally muttered.

She seemed to be acting strange and I became more and more paranoid as I followed her out of the cafe, wondering if she knew something. The smell of smoke still lingered on my shirt and I looked a complete mess, so I could hardly blame her for being blunt. Even still, her caginess unnerved me.

We crossed the road and when she pulled out a selection of keys from her jacket pocket, jangling them around, I flinched. She picked a gold one, twisted it in the keyhole and opened the door, then flicking on the lights and the air conditioning, motioned me to sit down. The scenario reminded me of when I'd met Carmela, the lawyer from the Spanish Consulate — the smart, attractive woman who had my fate and my future in her well-manicured hands.

There were three desks in total, two of them unoccupied. It was just the two of us in there. I looked around at the wall- to- wall posters, all of them advertising holiday destinations in Spain. In some, smiling Mums and Dads with their blissfully happy children played on white sandy beaches, while in others, couples held hands, strolling into their make-believe paradise. The headline of one poster caught my eye: 'Marbella, the holiday of a lifetime.' They couldn't have been more wrong. I sat there, lost in thought, trying to make sense of my time there.

The woman coughed to get my attention and I turned to face her.

"Can you confirm your name please?" she asked, her elbows propped up on her walnut desk and her hands clasped under her chin.

Taking off my sunglasses but with my cap firmly tilted downwards, I obliged, giving her my full name. Even though a cool breeze circulated around the room from the air conditioning purring away in the background, my heart was beating fast and sweat began to drip from my armpits and down my sides. She checked her paperwork while I sat there in turmoil.

"Yes, here it is; a single ticket to Gatwick. Is that correct?"

"Yes." I answered, both verbally and with a nod of the head.

"May I see you passport please?"

I reached across the desk and without a word handed it to her, aware that it was slightly damp due to holding it in my sweaty palm for too long.

How the fuck am I going to make it through passport control? I thought. I couldn't even deal with picking up my bloody ticket. My nerves were on a knife's edge and I swear I could feel my heart vibrating under my shirt.

"That's fine," she said, closing my passport and handing it to me.

I held my breath as she slid my ticket into a company envelope and passed it over.

"Thank you for your help," I said. I stood up shakily, replaced my sunglasses and made my way towards the door.

"Excuse me?"

With my hand on the door handle, I turned around and stared at her through the darkness of my sunglasses.

"Yes?"

There was a pause. She fucking knows something, I swear she does. My paranoia took its hold and my stomach flipped.

"Have a good flight home," she said with a wry smile.

"Thank you very much." I opened the door, stepped outside and closed it behind me. A few feet up the road, and with a grin on my face, I raised the ticket to my lips and kissed it.

With everything but the map packed safely into my rucksack, I made my way out of the cul-de-sac and back through the narrow streets towards the town centre. The clock on the church wall told me it was eight minutes to four — just three hours to go. The market was still bustling with tourists and the queue at the bus station had dwindled down to just a handful of people waiting patiently in line. I only wished that I had some money, a few spare coins to catch a ride to the airport. Not for the first time I had an image of being in that hotel room, reaching out my hand and scooping the cash into my pocket. My mind flooded with thoughts of the fire, of the dead bodies in the hallway and for a moment I was lost, caught up in the nightmare and unable to think straight. I wandered over to a wooden bench and sat down with my breath shallow and the panic pulsating under my skin. Closing my eyes, the noise of the busy town evaporated into silence.

It was only when the church bells chimed four times that I found myself suddenly back in the bustle of the town with the images of the fire slipping away into the recesses of my mind. I unfolded the map and stared at it, my eyes following the wavy line of the route I had to take. The N-340 — the coastal road — was the quickest way.

"Fifteen fucking miles, Dave," I muttered to myself, the enormity of what was ahead of me registering as I calculated how long it would take me on foot. There was no way I could do it; no way anybody could do it. I had to get a lift; there was no choice. Without one, I was just hours away from a prison sentence.

I stood up, flung the rucksack over my shoulder, ran towards the road and adopted the position — arm outstretched, thumb in the air. The blisters on my feet began to sting, rubbing against the inside of my well-worn trainers as I marched the pavements, all the while the afternoon sun hammering down on me as the sweat poured out of my body. My shirt stuck to my skin and my jeans felt heavy, dragging against my legs. I looked behind me with each and every sound of an engine, pleading with over-exaggerated facial expressions and mouthing the word 'please' to every driver that passed. I stared at them through their windscreens, begging them to stop. But not one car did; there wasn't even a glance from a fellow human being.

I passed through the town of Carvajal with the roof of my mouth almost stuck to my tongue. I'd have done anything for a drink, anything to feel some moisture on my lips and liquid in my stomach. With shaky hands I scanned the map, tracing the three miles I'd walked. There were still twelve to go and it occurred to me that even if time had been on my side, it was highly unlikely that I'd physically be able to make it. I'd been dehydrated before, many times, after heavy nights on the town, but this was different. With each step I took, my body was crying out for me to stop and rest, to get the fuel I knew it needed. But I persevered, praying like I'd never prayed in my life.

It must have been a mile or so later when the sudden sound of a horn stopped me in my tracks. As I turned, dizzy with exhaustion, a white scooter sparkling under the sun came into focus, slowing down as it approached me. The driver pulled over next to the grass verge and, with the engine still running and balancing the scooter with his feet on the road, he asked where I was going.

"Malaga airport," I told him, with the hope in me building to such an extent I thought I was going to burst. "My flight to Gatwick leaves at seven."

"I lived in London for two years, Camden Town... a great place to live. We..."

"Where're you headed now?" I asked, cutting him off in mid flow. I knew Camden well of course, but really didn't have the time or the inclination to strike up a conversation.

"Los Alamos. Any good?"

I shrugged my shoulders. "Is it anywhere near the airport?"

"About three miles away, give or take."

I almost hugged him. "Fantastic," I said. "How long will it take?"

"About half an hour on this thing," he joked, handing me the spare helmet that had been hooked over his handlebar.

I took off my cap, zipped it into my rucksack and strapped the helmet under my chin before climbing onto the bike.

The noise of the engine made conversation pretty impossible but that suited me fine. The last thing I felt capable of was a chat. With my hands gripping the side handles firmly and allowing the weight of the helmet to tilt my head back onto my shoulders, I basked in the joy of finally having a cool breeze in my face. Lost in thought, villages passed me by in a blur — Benalmadena, Puebio Monterrey and then Arroyo de la Miel — tranquil looking places in comparison to the mayhem of Marbella. I wondered what it was about me that had drawn me to Marbella in the first place and why I'd always felt the

need to be at the centre of things in crazy, wild places. Admittedly, I'd
been itching to feel the blood pumping through my veins again after
the few months of staying with my parents, when the daily routines
had become mind-numbingly tedious. But right then, I couldn't have
wished for anything more than to be back in London, back in their
home, with the knowledge that the milk would be on the doorstep at
seven and coffee would be in the pot by seven fifteen.

We came to a roundabout and took the first exit, and then a few
yards down the road we pulled over and stopped.

"Los Alomos," the driver said over the hum of the engine, looking
over his shoulder at me. "Just walk back up to the main road mate
and you're back on track for the airport."

Swinging my leg over the seat, I dismounted the bike, but my
rucksack fell awkwardly on my back, sliding to one side, and I swayed
on my feet.

"Thanks so much," I told him, wrestling with the buckle under
my chin. For a moment I felt dizzy again as I pulled off the helmet
and handed it to him. I breathed heavily in through my nose in an
attempt to get some air and re-adjusted the bag on my back but
the dizziness remained. I crouched over with my hands on my knees,
desperately trying to pull myself together.

"Are you alright, mate?"

"Yeah...," I said, "...I'll be fine." I stood up and the blood rushed
straight to my head. "Shit."

"Hey! Take it easy!"

I got my bearings and stood up, looking around me. I felt sick and
my legs were wobbling; I really felt awful.

"I don't suppose you could..."

"Get on," he said, handing me back the helmet and starting up
the engine.

We reached the airport in a matter of minutes and he pulled up
just yards away from the main entrance. I got off the bike and sat
down on the verge, taking everything in as I handed back the helmet.

"Are you sure you're ok?" he said.

"Far better than I would have been if you hadn't stopped," I told him, trying to laugh.

"Anything I can do?"

"You've done more than enough. Thank you."

I reached out my right hand and he shook it firmly. "Have a good flight, buddy."

Within seconds he was gone, back down the road and queuing at the roundabout.

I sat there for a few moments, gathering myself together, then stood up and made my way cautiously to the main doors. With my head down and my cap and glasses back on, my eyes were flitting everywhere — picking out people with suitcases on their way to check in and more people who had just arrived, congregating in the roadside. Policemen were stationed outside both the arrival and departure entrances, looking every bit as intimidating as they intended to be with their pistols strapped into holsters by their sides. Most were smoking and in deep conversation with their colleagues, but a few were looking out, ever observant, monitoring the motorists pulling up outside.

I walked between two rows of taxis waiting for fares, counting the paving slabs in front of me. There were fifteen slabs between me and the glass fronted sliding doors and in front of them were three policemen, standing to attention. My heart was in my throat, constricting it and unsettling me. I paused, trying to regulate my breathing, fumbling around with my rucksack, trying to blend in. I kept glancing up, waiting for them to be distracted by something or somebody else, and when an engine roared in the distance — a plane hurtling down the runway — I almost willed myself on it, desperate to get through those doors.

As I approached the policemen, taking huge breaths in and out, one of them suddenly moved. I froze on the spot, certain he was heading my way, but he ambled over to a car pulled up in the drop off area and leant over to speak with the driver through his window. The other two policemen started chatting; their backs towards me, and I watched as one took a cigarette packet from his trouser pocket.

I took my chance and strode towards the doors, reaching them just as the second policeman flicked his lighter. The automatic doors slid open and I stepped into the bright, air conditioned building, mingling with the crowds, unable to believe I'd managed to make it past them.

I headed straight for the toilet, weaving my way through the crowds and barging straight through the door. I lowered my head at the sink, gulping back unsafe water that I knew I shouldn't be drinking. The sensation of it sliding down my throat was incredible and I drank until I couldn't swallow another drop.

Back outside, I pulled my ticket and passport from my rucksack, glancing around to find my check-in point. And that's when I saw it — the large, digital clock on the main foyer wall. It was ten past six and I felt the hairs on the back of my neck stand up as I stared at it.

Fuck.

My thoughts turned to the apartment I'd left behind and to Paul, who right at that very moment was undoubtedly cursing me for being ten minutes late.

As I approached the check-in desk, I wondered how long it would take him to work out I wasn't going back... how long it would take for him to find my passport gone and to pick up his phone.

Chapter 22

WHITE LINES

The thought that Paul would discover his own passport on the bedside table instead of my own made my head spin. I lined up behind a queue of people feeling like I'd keel over at any moment, the hum of chatter around me becoming an unbearable drone in my head.

"Hurry the fuck up," I said through gritted teeth, standing behind a woman struggling with her two young children and their overweight suitcases. As much as I tried to focus on the task in hand, I couldn't keep still and my eyes flitted across hundreds of nameless faces, searching for Paul's, convinced he was going to show up. There were police on three sides of the building, their stark uniforms standing out amongst the colours in the crowds, and I watched them all as my queue shortened, ready to make my escape if they so much as moved in my direction. My mind was pumped and ready to run but my body was fucked; I knew I wouldn't even stand a chance. I talked myself into a panic, trying to find a solution to every possible scenario in my head, but I came up with nothing. I thought back to my time in the cell, the stink of piss, the prisoners glaring through the bars, all sense of humanity gone.

Dave, stay calm. Just collect your boarding pass and get on the fucking plane.

If getting past the check-in desk wasn't terrifying enough, I knew

I'd still have to get through passport control. I may as well have had a sign on my head that said: ARREST ME NOW because I'd never felt so conspicuous in my life.

My mind spiraled completely out of control. I glared at every person who so much as looked in my direction, and there were quite a few of them. I could smell my own sweat; smell the leftover smoke from the fire lodging in my nostrils. I smelt my own fear and felt it in my gut with every step I took towards the counter.

The queue in front of me slowly dispersed and I inched my way forward until finally the only thing between me and the dark-haired check-in girl was her white, melamine desk. I handed her my ticket and passport, warily took off my glasses and placed them on the counter. I stared at her, every bone in my body willing her to be at the end of her shift, too tired to question anything, too dumb to want to.

Be an airhead....go on...give me the same, stupid spiel you give them all.

"Any luggage sir?" she said, opening my passport and then tucking a loose strand of hair behind her ear.

"No, no, just hand luggage," I replied, lifting up my rucksack with one hand as I wiped beads of sweat from my forehead with the other.

She looked at my passport, looked at me, then back at the passport again. Closing it with a phony smile, she handed it back together with my boarding pass.

"Have you had a nice trip?"

What was this — twenty fucking questions? I smiled at her, aware I didn't look like I'd had the average package holiday.

"Yes. Lovely, thanks." What more could I say? I fidgeted, unable to look her directly in the eyes, willing her to move on.

"Your flight's on time, Sir, and due to leave in forty five minutes. You can make your way to the terminal."

"Thank you." I took my card and left the desk, but no more than four or five steps away from her, she spoke again.

"Excuse me sir..."

A sick feeling washed over me and I held my breath, slowly twisting my neck to look at her.

"Don't forget your sunglasses." She had them in her hands, leaning over the counter to hand them to me.

Giving a halfhearted smile in return, I walked away, slipping them back on, my head a complete mess.

Come on Dave, keep it together.

It felt like being a fugitive on the run.

Dave, you ARE on the fucking run I told myself, striding through the crowds to the terminal.

On my way, something caught my eye. To my right, I spotted a newspaper on top of one of the plastic red chairs that lined the length of the waiting area. The closer I got, the bolder the headline became and then staring straight at me were those words again:

I STEPPED OVER DEAD BODIES TO LOOT

"Is someone fucking playing with me?" I said out loud, looking around as the paranoia suffocated me. I hurriedly snatched up the paper and tossed it into the nearest bin.

You bastard Paul; you two faced fucking bastard.

My panic rocketed as I approached passport control and took my place behind three small groups of passengers. The guy behind the glass checked each passenger's passport and one by one they went through.

This is it Dave... it's now or never.

The man nodded for me to move forwards and I took five steps, crossing the white painted line on the floor with the fear and dread coursing through my body in a sickening rush. I was aware I was breathing far too heavily and my stomach churned, my heart slamming against my rib cage as a cold sweat consumed me.

We came face to face.

I slid my passport under the gap at the bottom of the glass screen and watched as he took it in his hands and opened it. My head was pounding and I started to shake as he stared at my photo. He pointed to me to remove my sunglasses, which I did, trying to keep my hand from trembling as I slipped them into my shirt pocket. Turning away, he looked down, checking a list on his desk. I was scared, really fucking scared, and stood there just waiting for him to signal to the police to come over and arrest me. The seconds passed by and I thought that at any moment he'd see my name on his list and I'd feel the hand of the law on my heavy shoulders.

Stay calm, Dave. Just hold it together.

He looked up, staring at me intensely, his eyes digging into mine as the adrenalin raced inside me and whooshed around my head. He looked at the passport again, and then at me again, with piercing eyes that didn't flinch.

You're fucking playing with me, you bastard.

He just kept staring at me, unblinking, his black pupils dilated, and I could hear my heart throbbing in my ears. I was prepared for the worst — ready for it — but then he snapped my passport closed, pushed it through the gap and nodded for me to move on.

I was too stunned to be ecstatic. I'd made it through, and of course I wanted to jump for fucking joy, but there was a huge part of me that didn't believe it was even possible to leave a country under such circumstances. Were they crazy? Didn't they have the slightest idea what was going on around them? I had to stay calm — stay focused until I was on that plane and on my way home — but by now I had so many thoughts in my head I was close to losing the plot completely.

They're gonna get you on that plane, Dave. Just you wait. The further they let you get, the more they'll charge you with. They're biding their time... they're watching you.

Moments later I handed my boarding pass to another member of airport security who tore off the stub, returned the pass and waved me on. I ran down the corridor, overtaking the other passengers, and jumped onto the waiting bus that was taking us to the plane. As we drove the short distance, the harrowing feeling that I still wouldn't make it consumed me.

The bus came to a halt and the doors slid open. I waited for a number of passengers to step off first and then I jumped out, losing myself amongst the crowd as we made our way across the small stretch of tarmac to the plane's steps. It was like being caught up in a snowball, being pushed along, with no sense of direction. One by one the people climbed the steps to the entrance, but I held back, not wanting to be caught up in a queue I couldn't escape from. When they were clear, I dashed up the steps, turning to take one final look around, just to make sure Paul or the police weren't on my trail. I showed my boarding pass to the air hostess who welcomed me on board, noted my seat number and directed me to the end of the aircraft. Strolling down the narrow aisle past all the seated passengers, I felt their eyes on me and my paranoia kicked in again. But who could blame them for staring? Looking disheveled with a ripped, dirty shirt and undoubtedly wafting lingering smells of smoke and perspiration in their direction, I lowered my head and made my way to the end.

I'd been given a window seat, the only one empty in a row of three, next to a young couple who were already seated. They stood up as I squeezed past them and with great relief I sat down, finally resting my exhausted and mentally drained body.

A beam of light from the early evening sun shone through the small window making a warm square on the leg of my jeans. I looked out over the runway with wide eyes still on alert as the captain intro-duced himself and his crew. He announced that we'd be taking off within a few minutes and that the journey to Gatwick would take approximately two hours and forty minutes. Seeing nothing out of the ordinary outside — nothing to alarm me — I let my head fall back against the seat and I closed my eyes, trying my best to blank out the chatter and movement of the other passengers. Hearing the stewardess' pull the doors closed, I opened my eyes and breathed deeply, knowing that within minutes, I'd be on my way home.

They performed their standard routine of showing us what to do if we nose-dived into the open seas below; how to use the life jackets under our seats and the oxygen masks above. They pointed to the exit doors — at the front, the centre and the rear — and finally made their way along the aisle to check that our seat belts were secure. When

I felt movement beneath me, it couldn't have come quickly enough, and peering through the window, I watched the black tarmac being left behind. The plane picked up speed and the noise of the roaring engine, the sensation of being pushed back against my seat and finally being lifted into the fading blue sky, was unbelievable.

I leant my head against the window and stared out at the darkening sky as we rose above the clouds. All I could think of was seeing Dad at the airport; of embracing him and not letting go.

I'd done it. I'd actually, fucking done it.

As we soared higher in the sky, I thought of England, visualizing all the people and places I knew and loved.

And then it hit me.

Before I could even wrap my arms around Dad or do any of the things I was dreaming of, I still had to get through passport control on the other side. I was stupid enough to believe that it was almost over, when in reality, it had only just begun.

Chapter 23

PERFUMES AND AFTERSHAVES

Turbulence suddenly shook me and I awoke disorientated, but the plane was still; the unbalance was within. Catching my breath and sparing a glance out to the other passengers, I clocked the watch on my neighbour's wrist: seven forty five. There was just under an hour to go.

The couple beside me still had their heads in their paperbacks, in fact the only time they'd put them down was to change the time on their watches, rewinding them an hour in preparation for our arrival in the UK. We hadn't had one conversation — not because I was being unsociable but because I felt humiliated and embarrassed by my appearance.

Staring at nothing but my reflection bouncing back at me from the square window and with only the navy blue sky as background, my mood lifted in anticipation of seeing Dad at the airport. I wandered what he may be going through as he drove to pick me up and whether or not he was alone. Perhaps he was chatting to Mum, to Pink or one my brothers? I hoped he had someone with him — I really didn't want to face him alone.

Words floated around my mind in an attempt to form sentences as I contemplated what I'd say when I saw him. I wasn't sure if words would even be necessary — the guilt was etched clearly across my face.

"We have a full range of perfumes, aftershaves, toys and watches," the pretty blonde airhostess said in her cute, Irish accent as she pushed the trolley of goodies past me. I declined of course, having no money at all on me. In fact I hadn't had any for days, for weeks. The guy next to me turned a page of his book, ignoring her, and his wrist twisted towards me. I checked the time again, straining my eyes to see the numbers pinpointed by the tube of light funneling itself from the dashboard above. It was seven fifty seven.

Adjusting myself in my seat, my brain was a mash of thoughts. It felt like my head had been split, sliced open with a razor sharp knife, and all my thoughts careered off in different directions. Feelings of being happy, sad, frightened and lonely crashed into each other and snowballed.

As the plane began to descend, 1 felt a tingling feeling rushing through my body from my head to my toes as the nerves and anxiety took over. My dirty finger nails tasted vile as I chipped away at them.

This is it Dave, you're so fucking close.

I continued to chew the nail of my index finger on my left hand.

I wonder if Dad is already there?

A slight crackle came from the speaker overhead and a severe shot of pain stretched along my head and down the side to my ears as the plane descended rapidly. For a second, as the Captain spoke, I mentally wandered in my own world and got caught within my thoughts.

Ladies and gentleman, this is the Captain speaking. We have a fugitive on the plane and I must ask you ALL to stay seated after we have landed.

I tried to the rub away the immense pain from my ears with the knuckles of my fists as the Captain spoke.

"Ladies and gentlemen, this is the Captain speaking. I'm delighted to inform you we are on schedule and will be arriving at Gatwick on time. The temperature is seven degrees with a nasty westerly chill and a little drizzle. I would advise a jumper or jacket for when you step off the plane."

A jumper or jacket? If only...

There was a string of moans and groans from some of the passengers. "Typical bloody English weather," barked a man two rows down, sharing his frustration whilst speaking over the voice coming through the speakers.

"I hope you have enjoyed the flight, thank you for choosing our airline and have a safe journey to your next destination." His microphone clicked off and his colleagues strolled down the aisle for the final time with plastic bags collecting any rubbish, sweet wrappers, polystyrene cups and newspapers.

Above me the seat belt light sprang into action, informing us to buckle up, but there was no need — I'd had my belt wrapped around my waist throughout the flight. Somehow it had made me feel safer.

The male steward unhooked the microphone from its bracket. "We will be making our decent into Gatwick Airport in approximately six minutes. Please make sure your seat belts are fastened and your trays are clear and in an upright position."

"Six minutes." I repeated under my breath. "Six minutes."

The plane tilted slightly to the left and began a slow and steady turn. Down below, with the glittering of street lights, the ground looked like square plots on a map. Gradually, even in the darkening sky, everything began to come into view as we neared the ground — small cars with their bright lights heading down the motorways and through the maze of country lanes that weaved between various homes of different sizes and shapes.

A sudden bump told me the landing gear had been released. My ears popped as I opened my mouth to release the pressure. Trees and rooftops whizzed by as the aircraft made its final turn onto the waiting runway and there was a deep rumbling as the tyres seduced the tarmac. A loud rush of air giving pressure to the brakes slowly brought the plane to the speed of a motor bike, culminating into the final act of taxiing slowly into the arrival gate.

As the plane came to a standstill, I stared out of the window, watching the rain drops race each other down the glass pane.

Am I really here? I rubbed my face then squeezed my eyes until I saw a kaleidoscope of patterns and colours.

The flashing light above indicated that we could release out seat belts. People began to stand and open the overhead lockers to retrieve their hand luggage but I sat looking at the floor with relentless thoughts flying through my head. Drops of sweat fell and submerged into my jeans.

Come on Dave, one more hurdle, that's it, that's all. It sounded easy but I was so fucking scared — I had visions of the police waiting for me as I stepped off the plane.

The doors opened and people slowly moved down the aisle with their possessions and one by one thanked the aircrew before stepping into the dark and drizzly UK weather.

Still seated, I grabbed the rucksack from the floor and straightened my cap. Taking a deep breath of air, I rose from the seat, side stepped across the two people next to me and pigeon stepped behind the remaining passengers. I felt numb with fear. With every step I took towards the exit, my blood pumped violently into my limbs, the panic taking its hold.

"Thank you for flying with us," the steward said and I faked a smile, nervously looking to my left to see if any other uniformed personnel were waiting to show their appreciation.

As I took my first stride onto the metal steps, raindrops splattering onto my shirt, I looked around. Even in the low lit darkness I couldn't see any police, just fellow passengers and airport crew directing us to the waiting bus. We all got on and I mingled within the crowd. Trying to control my breathing as we were driven to the entrance of the airport, I was confused, unable to comprehend why I hadn't been grabbed.

They must be waiting for me inside.

The glass fronted doors slid open and like a pack of obedient dogs we followed the florescent signs through the corridors of the airport to passport control. I felt like turning back, even hiding behind a vending machine, but there was no turning back now, nowhere to hide.

Feeling a sudden surge in my stomach, I ran to the bathroom, kicked the cubicle door with my foot and threw the rucksack on the floor. Lifting the seat, I took a deep breath, opened my mouth as wide as I could and slid my finger down my throat. The acrid smell of vomit filled my nostrils as I heaved rancid, runny mucus into the toilet bowl. Saliva followed in dribs and drabs as I coughed and splattered nothing but liquid substance from my body.

Wiping my mouth with the back of my hand I stood at the row of basins. Running the tap, I cupped handfuls of water and splashed my flushed face several times, letting the coldness wash over me.

It's time to face the music, Dave.

I stared at my reflection, my pupils dilating in rhythm with my pulse dancing under my skin. I tucked my shirt into my jeans, closed the tap, removed my cap and stared again at my gaunt, frightened face in the mirror. All I wanted was to see Dad waiting for me in the arrivals lounge but I was terrified. I blew air in and out of my mouth, trying to control my breathing, then after drying my face and hands, I threw the damp paper towel in the silver bin and opened the door.

Fewer people were making their way to passport control. I trailed behind them, my mind bursting with unrelenting thoughts.

Let me through. Please... just let me through.

I stood nervously with a queue of people before me, waiting behind the white line. I felt like giving up, just giving in, as again, sickness began to form a solid mixture within me. The queue shortened as one by one the people were let through. And then it was my turn... my turn to step over the chipped painted line that ran across the width of the room.

"May I see you passport please," the uniformed man behind the glass said. His voice was stern, his face expressionless.

I pushed my passport through the gap and he opened it up and stared at my photo. I watched him, his eyes widening. Or was I seeing things? He looked up towards me.

"On your own sir?" he said.

I began to rub my moist hands nervously together. "Yes, just me," I replied as I smelt the stale lingering smell of smoke wafting from my clothes.

He must be able to smell it? He's bound to notice.

I watched him flick through the pages of my passport.

"Been away for some time, have you?" He turned each and every page, studying them.

"A month or so."

Just be cool, Dave. But I was far from being cool and I felt my whole body sliver into a furnace of heat. He knows something, he fucking does. Just get it over and done with and detain me... get me out of my misery.

"Thank you Sir. Have a safe trip home," he said, sliding my passport back under the gap.

Is that it? No police? No arrest? Nothing? My body shook with excitement as I strolled through the 'nothing to declare' section, but it was short-lived. I still had premonitions that the police would be waiting for me at the arrival hall and pounce on me as I reached Dad's outstretched arms.

The sliding doors opened and in front of me was a mass of people. I searched for Dad but couldn't see him, just taxi drivers with names in black thick lines scrawled across cardboard, people leaning against steel rails waiting to meet and greet their loved ones. Then I saw them; Dad and Pink.

"Yes my sister's here!" I said, punching the air, before realising I was drawing attention to myself. I lowered my head, waiting for something to happen, but it didn't. And then Pink spotted me. She pointed, and then nudged Dad, and their eyes never left me as I made my way over to them.

"Dave, you're here!" she said hysterically in between sobs, her tears running down her cheeks and taking her black mascara with them. She embraced me and kissed my ashamed face as I nestled my head on her shoulder. I didn't want to let go. My eyes were closed but I was still thinking that at any moment there'd be a firm hand on my back from the law. I finally pulled away, my tearful eyes looking into hers and registering the confusion of pain and happiness I saw in them. She said nothing; she didn't need to.

I turned to face Dad, seeing the concern etched across his tired, handsome face. "Bloody hell, look at the state of you," he said, pulling me from my sister, taking me in his arms and wrapping them tightly around me. "What the hell's happened to you?" Tears rolled from his eyes and down his face, dampening mine. I'd never seen him cry before. He held me for a few moments, sobbing into my shoulder and then I lifted my head to look at him. I held his face firmly in my hands, covering his wet cheeks, and wiped away his tears with my thumbs.

"Dad," I choked, struggling to get the words out as the emotion took hold of me. "I'm so sorry for putting you through this. I'm just so sorry."

He took hold of me again. "At least you're home, son," he said. "At least you're home."

Chapter 24

TWENTY ONE YEARS

Rain lashed against the windows as I unwrapped the aluminium foil packet which Pink had handed me. It was a sandwich from Mum. "He'll be starving," Mum had told them. And she was right, I was.

"So how is Mum?" Even though I knew the answer, I had to ask.

Dad didn't say a word.

"She's not great Dave, but what did you expect?" Pink pressed the switch to open the passenger window slightly. "You know what she's like; she's been so worried about you." She turned to look at me. "When was the last time you had a wash or a change of clothes? In fact, where are your clothes? Where's your suitcase?"

I shoved my head in the gap between the two front seats, trying to block out the sound of the rain. "I had to leave the case with the owner at this hostel. I owed him rent, so he kept my case with all my stuff until I paid him. But I had no money, so I couldn't pay him and I lost the bloody lot."

She shook her head. "So what's in the rucksack?"

"Nothing; just an empty carton I used for water, and a map. That's it. I've been wearing these clothes for days...since the fire."

Sue turned to look at Dad, he looked at her, and they both shook their heads simultaneously.

There was a pause in the conversation as the heavy rain pelted against the windscreen. Sitting back and finishing off the sandwich, I lay across the seat, pushed the rucksack under my head and closed my eyes.

"Okay son, nearly home," Dad quietly said as he looked at me through the rear view mirror.

"Dad...about the ticket..."

His eyes met mine. "Forget it son. Anyone would have done the same."

The journey passed by in a blur. I was stretched across the back seat, doing my best to answer the questions Dad and Pink had for me. I told them everything that had happened and when the conversation lulled to a silence, I slept.

It was an hour or so later when Pink nudged me awake and I looked up to see the familiar apartment block where my parents lived.

Pink opened the car door, got out and covered her brown wavy hair with her coat to protect herself from the downpour. Opening the passenger door I felt nervous about seeing Mum. Dad was always the strict one of the two but now the tables had turned and on this occasion he was the calmer one. I liked that; I needed him.

As we walked to their apartment where Mum and Dad had lived for the past few years since selling the family home, I stood for a moment and looked up to the sky as the raindrops continued to fall. Strangely, I'd missed it, and with nothing but sun and heat for a month, I enjoyed it pleasuring my face.

Following behind Dad and Sue to the main door, I had a tremendous bout of remorse. I was shaking with a combination of emotions as I carried my guilt ridden body up the two flights of stairs to their apartment on the second floor.

"You okay Dave? You look like you've seen a ghost?" Sue said as I leant against the wall whilst Dad fumbled with the key in the lock.

"Not really," I said. "I'm knackered." I stared down at my feet. "I feel so ashamed about what I've put everyone through."

Sue wrapped her arms around my waist. I towered over her — she was only around five feet tall, just like Mum.

"I haven't even told you half the things that I went through."

"You're back now," she said, "with your family. No more tears, okay?"

Dad opened the door, hung his damp coat up on the hook in the hallway, went inside and left Sue and I talking.

"It's not over you know, Sue. I left. . . I did a bloody runner. They're bound to come looking for me. It's been in all the papers. . . people know me. Shit, it's never ending."

"We'll help you, okay? In time Dave, this will be all forgotten. You'll see. . . it will." She removed her arms from my waist and placed her coat on a hook next to Dads.

"Sue?"

She turned round to look at me, "Yes?"

"Is Mum okay? Really, is she?"

"As I said, she's been worried sick. You're her son and she's been crying bucket loads and at the same time trying to be strong. She's had to go to work as well through this — we all have — with people asking questions every day." She turned around, nodding her head towards the living room. "You coming?"

"Yep, give me a minute."

"Okay." She pushed the front door to. "I'll phone your brothers to tell them you're home."

"Thanks," I said. "Send them my love."

I threw the rucksack onto the communal hallway floor and wiped away the tears before looking at myself in the bronze mirror in the hallway. It belonged to Nan and Pop, Mums parents. They'd passed away about ten years before. They were beautiful people.

I studied my face, the face that I was ashamed of, the face that has caused so much sorrow to my family. I couldn't bear it — couldn't bear to see the person I'd become. I flicked my eyes to the left, away from my reflection, focusing on the ornate swirls in the mirror's frame. I'd always loved it, this mirror. It wasn't so much the design of it, but the thought that so many people I loved and cared about had stood before it, looking into it. I often thought about the secrets it held.

Something triggered in my memory, a faraway thought of words I'd spoken just a few months before. I thought of Mrs. Evans, the woman whose house I'd been selling, the one who was reluctant to part with her hallway mirror.

"It's just a mirror," I'd told her.

"But a rather nice one, don't you think?" she'd said.

"I guess it depends who's looking into it. I think a mirror is only as beautiful as its beholder."

I turned back to my reflection, half expecting the glass to shatter into a million pieces, unable to welcome my face. But the glass remained — solid, unwavering, accepting; just as my family had.

"I hate you," I said, looking into my own eyes before turning away in disgust.

When I opened the living room door and saw that nothing had changed, it made me smile. Sue was sitting with a cup of coffee on the three-seater settee against the wall under the large double glazed window. Mum was on the matching two-seater against the other wall and Dad was sitting in his chair between them both, his hot cup of tea on the small black shelf fitted on the wall above the electric wall heater. The three glassed-topped triangle coffee tables housed an array of nuts and raisins in matching dishes. There were always goodies to eat at Mums.

Mum looked at me as I walked in and automatically burst into tears. "Oh my God Dave, look at you... you're all skin and bones."

I walked over and sat next to her, put my arm around her shoulder as my tears made another appearance.

"Mum, I'm so sorry, I really am." I tried to talk, tried to explain what had happened but I didn't know where to start, I couldn't think, couldn't get the words out. I was just so happy and grateful to be home. I kissed her on her cheek and gave her a big cuddle. "Mum, I love you."

"I love you too darling," she said, her soft, gentle voice barely audible between the sobs. "Thank God you're here, but Dave... we've been so worried. You in prison, the papers, you've really sha......"

"I know Mum, I know," I interrupted, not wanting to hear the words, not wanting to hear what I'd done to them.

A few minutes passed in silence, no one really knowing what to say, and no one really knowing where to start. Mum and I just held each other whilst Dad watched the snooker on the television, the sound at a level where he could just about hear what the commentators were saying.

Mum broke the silence. "I'll get you something to eat," she said. "It's ready in the fridge. We can talk after." She was just about to stand when Dad interrupted.

"No. Let him get it, you've done enough."

Dad was like that — he'd say his piece which we all listened to and then he'd sit in his chair in the corner, cigarette in hand, in a world of his own.

"Mum, he's right. Don't worry, I'll get it okay? You sit."

"No, you sit Dave. I'll get it." Sue stood up and walked to the kitchen and Dad rolled his eyes, sighing as he exhaled a large cloud of smoke.

I didn't know what to do or say and sat there for a few moments, unable to look at the TV that Dad was staring at, unable to look at the empty space in the middle of the room that Mum seemed to be staring at.

"I'm gonna have a shower," I said, "And get these bloody clothes off. I'll be ten minutes."

"Okay darling," Mum said. "There's a towel in the airing cupboard."

"I know. Thanks."

I got up and walked to my old bedroom.

Everything looked the same, eerily so, as if nothing at all had happened. As I showered I wondered how long it would take for me to feel a part of it all again and whether a knock on the door would come before I even had the chance to try and make things right.

Having put on clean clothes for the first time in ages, I went back to join my family and ate my meal, devouring each mouthful far quicker than I knew was sensible. If indigestion was the only thing I'd have to worry about though, I'd be a lucky man.

"That was lovely, Mum. Boy, I've missed your cooking."

She smiled at me as I placed the cutlery in the middle of the empty plate.

"Do you mind if I crash? I'm so tired. I just need to lay on something comfortable... it's been a long, long day."

"Of course, it's late anyway," Mum said. "I have the day off tomorrow, so we'll talk then."

I pushed the dining room chair under the table and reached down to give Mum a hug. She held me tight as I kissed her goodnight, and again I felt the sting of tears in my eyes.

Pink stood up to leave too, walking towards me to hug me. I let go of Mum and held my sister, squeezing her tight.

"I'll see you tomorrow," she said, wiping her eyes. "Just having you here now... it's..." Her voice trailed off.

"I'm not going anywhere, Sue," I told her.

After kissing Mum and Dad goodbye, she closed the door behind her. I gave Dad a kiss and a hand shake, looking into his eyes, silently thanking him for all he'd done.

I left them and sank into bed wondering about the mess I'd left behind between them in the living room, but within a couple of minutes I was asleep.

There was a gentle tap on the door. "Dave, you awake?"

"Yes Mum, just resting."

I'd been woken up about ten minutes earlier by the sound of the morning rain hitting the window, surprised I'd slept for so long. I tried to put what had happened into some kind of perspective, but everything was still an ugly mess of disconnected thoughts.

Mum came in with a mug of coffee and some hot, buttered toast.

"Here you are, darling," she said placing it on the bedside table under the window.

"Thanks Mum," I said. "It sure beats oranges and water." I smiled — a thin smile — trying to make light of it.

"Dad told me everything," she said. "I just can't believe it."

I propped myself up on one elbow and took a mouthful of coffee, relishing the feeling of it sliding down my throat and warming me from the inside.

"You know how I heard about it, don't you?" she went on.

"Yes, Bob told me. I'm so sorry, Mum; I don't know what to say."

"I know you've been through a lot," she said, her voice firmer now. "But you've shamed us. You know that, don't you?"

I opened my mouth to speak but she carried on.

"Our name's been plastered all over the papers. People are still talking about it. First drink driving and getting arrested for that, then losing your job and your home..."

She was getting angrier; her voice rising to a level I wasn't used to. I let her continue, unable to say anything or defend myself, not even wanting to.

"And now this, Dave." Her fingers were twitching, softly clenching into her palms as she grabbed the material on her dressing gown and twisted it around. "Prison. Can you imagine what people at work, here, everywhere, have been saying? You — my son — in prison for arson and manslaughter. Dave, how could you get involved in all of this?"

Putting down the half empty mug of coffee on the bedside table, I slid under the duvet, ashamed. I was so full of complete and utter guilt.

"And Dad," she went on. "What he went through to get that ticket."

"I know Mum," I told her, the words catching in my throat and losing themselves in the thickness of the covers.

Dad had saved me, I knew that. And I knew exactly what he'd risked in doing so. He'd had every reason to turn his back on me and walk away — every reason to cast me from the family. But he hadn't. None of them had.

The tears flowed freely, streaming down my face, disappearing into the warmth of the sheets. Mum sat at the end of the bed, her silence speaking more words than if she'd opened her mouth. I felt her place her hand on my leg; a firm indication that she wasn't about to leave me. She never would; I knew that. And somehow it made me feel like that no matter what happened, I'd be ok.

It would be ok.

"Dad told me you saved two people's lives."

I waited for a moment, bringing alive the images in my mind. "Yes," I told her. "I did." My thoughts of them vanished and were immediately replaced with images of the charred, dead bodies, burnt in front of me on the floor, the ones I didn't save, the ones I couldn't.

"I've put your clothes in the bin. They're gone now."

"Mum..."

"They were ruined, Dave. They stank of smoke. You can get others."

I eased myself from under the covers and sat up, the duvet wrapped around my waist. Mum looked at me, tears beginning to show, trying to deal with her own guilt.

"I couldn't come to the airport," she said, her voice faltering. "I wanted to, I was more or less out the door with them, but I was so angry, so upset." Her voice softened. "Dave, you're my son. I'm so happy you're here and I love you so much but..."

I took hold of her hand, my heart breaking.

"...I love you, son, but what have you done?"

Outside, the sun rose, and a solitary milk cart made its way down the road, the gentle whir and hum of its engine breaking the silence. In the distance, early birds flew through the skies, their squawks and calls cutting through the dawn.

"Mum?"

She looked at me, her face as beautiful as it ever was but the sadness lodged in every fold of her skin.

"Yes Darling?" Her soft eyes looked at me and her head tilted slightly, just to the left, so half of her face was in the light of the morning sun.

"Come here," I said, and she moved towards me, reaching out, taking me into her arms as she had done for all of her life.

"You know...I just want to be normal... just like everyone else."

After that, there were no words. The birds flew by, and the milk float made its way to the end of the street, and the sun rose in the sky and my Mum continued to hold me, not for a moment letting go.

I'd made it home.

But in twenty years, I've never — not for a single second — forgotten about the ones who didn't.

AFTERWORD

Thank you for buying and reading my story. I hope you enjoyed it as much as I had the pleasure in writing it. Even though I'm not a writer, I needed to get this story out of my system; not just to prove my innocence, but to get it out in the open. The newspaper headlines were damming and they still continue to haunt me. Someone once told me that things are better out than in.

Since this happened at the beginning of the nineties, I've spent my life looking over my shoulder. Unbelievably, I haven't had any communication at all from anyone; not from the Spanish or the UK police, nor from Paul or the court.

I haven't been back to Spain since the day I left, but I've been to many countries since. Even though I always fear the worse, I haven't had one problem with passport control or security. I've endured many sleepless nights though, and still have nightmares about everything that happened. It's been twenty years, but not a week goes by without me thinking of the two people I saved and the many more that I couldn't.

The images of the dead bodies in the hotel are etched in my mind and will be with me for as long as I live. Whenever I'm on my own at home, on my way to work, sitting looking out at the ocean or walking in the countryside, I reflect about what I went through. Sometimes it doesn't feel real, like it never happened. Maybe that's me just wishing it never did.

15630424R00113

Printed in Great Britain
by Amazon